Phone Numbers

School name, phone: _____

Teacher's name, phone: _____

School counselor name, phone: _____

School name, phone: _____

Teacher's name, phone: _____

School counselor name, phone: _____

Coach's name, phone: _____

Coach's name, phone: _____

Clubs or groups for teens:
Name: _____   Phone: _____
Name: _____   Phone: _____
Name: _____   Phone: _____
Name: _____   Phone: _____

Teen's friends:
Name: _____   Phone: _____
Name: _____   Phone: _____
Name: _____   Phone: _____
Name: _____   Phone: _____

Other phone numbers:
Name: _____   Phone: _____
Name: _____   Phone: _____
Name: _____   Phone: _____
Name: _____   Phone: _____

What To Do When Your Child Is Heavy

Easy to Read • Easy to Use

Gloria Mayer
Michael Villaire

Institute for Healthcare Advancement
501 S. Idaho St., Suite 300
La Habra, California 90631
(800) 434-4633

Institute for Healthcare Advancement
501 S. Idaho Street, Suite 300
La Habra, California 90631

Printed in the United States of America
14 13 12   6 5 4 3
ISBN: 978-0-9720148-4-7

To Our Readers

This book is for parents of children who are heavy. Heavy children have a higher chance of having bad health when they grow up. It is never too late for anyone to make changes in their life. We hope this book will help you and your family to make healthy lifestyle choices.

Read this book with your family or by yourself. It will tell you ways you can live a healthy life. A healthy lifestyle is for all your family. Work together on the things the book tells you.

Exercise, eating the right food, eating the right amount of food, drinking lots of water, and family support are all important to a healthy family. This book will tell you how you can do these things to be healthy.

If your child is heavy, you must talk to the doctor or nurse. They will help you. They will tell you how much your child should be eating each day. They will tell you which foods they should be eating. They will let you know if it is okay for them to exercise. Show them this book. Bring it with you to your child's doctor visits. Write down your questions. Write down what the doctor or nurse tells you to do.

If you are pregnant, be sure you keep a healthy weight. Work closely with your doctor and nurse. Breast feed your baby up to age 1. This will help your child grow up healthy.

To Our Readers

It can be hard to make healthy choices today. Life can get very busy. This book will help you. If you work together as a family, it will be easier.

Doctors and nurses have read this book. They agree that the things it tells you are safe and can help you and your heavy child. But each child is different. Listen to what your kid's doctor or nurse tells you to do.

Remember, all children have feelings. They need you to show them how to be healthy. This means that everyone in the family should eat healthy and exercise. Not just the heavy child. Love and support are very important.

What's in This Book

What's in This Book

Heavy Children

Notes

_____

_____

_____

_____

_____

_____

_____

_____

_____

_____

_____

_____

_____

_____

1

Who Is a Heavy Child?

What is it?

A heavy child weighs more than he should for his age, height and weight. Boys and girls weigh different, too. A heavy child has more body fat than a child needs. Some people use other words to talk about a heavy child. Your doctor may say your child is "overweight" or "obese." In this book we will use the word "heavy" to talk about children who weigh more than they should.

Did you know?

- There are many kids in the U.S. who are heavy. If you look at any 20 kids in the U.S., 3 or 4 of them will be heavy.

- Kids that are heavy have more chance of being heavy when they grow up.

- Heavy adults are more likely to get sick and be unhealthy. Helping your child now will help your child be a healthy adult.

- Doctors and nurses do not always tell you if your child is heavy. You must ask them if your child is heavy. Then ask them what to do.

- There are many ways to tell if your child is heavy. The best way is to look at your child and be honest. Parents are not helping their heavy children by saying they are not heavy.

Who Is a Heavy Child?

- Look at your child. Be honest. Does your child look heavy? Look at these pictures. Does your child look like these kids?

Look for these:

- Round face
- Fat around the waist and belly
- Skin folds around the wrists and elbows

- Use a growth chart to help you know if your child is a healthy weight. (See "Height and Weight Chart" on page 7.)

- There are other ways to tell when your child is heavy. Here are some things you may notice:

- Your child has trouble keeping up with other kids who are the same age.
- Your child gets out of breath when running and playing.

Who Is a Heavy Child?

- Your child likes to sit inside better than to play outdoors.
- Your child may have dark colored skin around their neck.
- Your child is shy and withdrawn around other kids.
- Your child wears clothes 2 sizes bigger than their age.

- Ask yourself: Is my child heavy? If the answer is "yes" you will need to learn how to help your child. In this book you will learn things to do and things not to do.

- There are ways doctors and nurses know if a kid is heavy. They use a BMI Chart. BMI stands for body mass index. The BMI is for kids over 2 years old. The BMI can be hard to understand. You can believe your doctor or nurse if they tell you that your child is heavy.

- If your child is heavy, there are many things you can do to help your child. Things written in this book will help your child be healthy.

What can I do?

- Read this book to find out what to do for your heavy child.

- Live an active and healthy life. Your children will see what you do and do what you do. Be a role model. This is the best way to help your kids.

- Find ways for your heavy child to be active.

- Teach your child to eat healthy food.

- Help your kids to have healthy food to eat. Do not cook food for your family that is not healthy.

- Do not overfeed your baby.

- Do the activities found in this book with your heavy kid.

Who Is a Heavy Child?

- Never call your child fat or other bad names. Do not let anyone tease your heavy child.

- Be careful how you talk about your heavy child's weight. Show that you support your heavy child. Say good things about your heavy child.

- Make a plan to work on your heavy child's weight.

- Do not talk to other people about your child's weight when your child can hear you.

- Make it important for your child to exercise, have friends, and do well in school.

- Let your heavy child know that you love him or her.

- Use this book to help your whole family live healthy lives. This will help everyone in your family not to be heavy.

When should I get help?

- You first think your child is heavy. Visit a doctor or nurse.

- Your heavy child is sick. Visit a doctor or nurse.

- Your heavy child is being teased at school. Visit your child's teacher or a counselor at school. Talk about what can be done to stop teasing.

- If you don't know what to do for your heavy child. Visit your doctor or nurse. Ask to be sent to someone who can help you.

- Ask your own doctor about how you can help your heavy child. He or she may know people who can help you to help your whole family be healthy.

Height and Weight Chart

What is it?

A height and weight chart shows you what is a normal height and weight for a child at each age.

Did you know?

- You can use a height and weight chart to help tell if your child is heavy.
- The chart will tell you the normal height and weight for your child at each age.
- Normal means what kids should weigh to be healthy.
- There is a chart for boys and a chart for girls. Boys and girls grow differently.
- Kids grow in spurts. They may be shorter or taller than the chart says they should be. They may weigh more than the chart says. This can change quickly in kids. Talk to your doctor or nurse if your child's height and weight does not match the chart.
- Things to think about when reading a height and weight chart:
  - Kids often get heavier right before a growth spurt.
  - Not all kids at the same age have the same body build. It is normal for some kids to be short or tall. Some kids have a larger body build.
  - A height and weight chart is one way to look at your child's weight.

Height and Weight Chart

- Your doctor or nurse has a growth chart that also uses BMI and percentiles.
    - BMI is short for "body mass index." It is a number that matches height and weight to see if a boy or girl is at a healthy weight for their age.
    - Percentile is a number based on 100 kids that tells if a kid at the same age is bigger or smaller.
- Your doctor or nurse uses growth charts to tell if your child is growing normally.
- Your doctor or nurse keeps records of the growth of your child. They will look at the growth of your child over months and years.

What can I do?

- Measure your child's height. Write the height on a calendar or in a notebook.
- To know how tall your child is, do the steps below. Try to do this on a hard floor like tile, not carpet:
    - Take off your child's shoes.
    - Have your child stand straight with heels against the wall.
    - Put the ruler flat on top of your child's head.
    - Make a pencil mark on the wall where the ruler touches. Make sure it is level.

- Measure from the floor up to the mark you made. This is the height of your child. Write this down so you know it next time.

- When a nurse measures your child, ask what the height is and write it down. Write down the date, too.

• Weigh your child. Write the weight on a calendar or in a notebook.

• To know what your child weighs:

- Use a bathroom scale.

- To get a correct weight:

  • The scale must be on a flat floor.

  • Your child must stand still on the scale.

- Weigh your child before breakfast.

- Weigh your child with shoes off.

- If you do not have a bathroom scale, use a scale at a drugstore or at a school. A friend may have a scale that you can use.

• Do not weigh your child every day. Do not let your child use the bathroom scales every day. A good rule is to weigh your child every month if your child is not heavy. Weigh your child once a week if they are heavy.

Height and Weight Chart

- Do not put a lot of attention on how much your child weighs. Knowing what your child weighs is only one way to see if your child is heavy.

- Look at a growth chart to see where your child is on the chart.

- To read a chart, put your finger on your child's age. Move your finger across the page to find the height in inches and normal weight in pounds. If your child is taller or shorter than the height you see here, ask your doctor or nurse which number to use. **If your child is older than 12, talk to your doctor or nurse.**

Height and Weight Chart for Girls

Age	Height	Weight
2 years	30 inches	26 to 31 pounds
3 years	33 inches	28 to 34 pounds
4 years	37 inches	32 to 39 pounds
5 years	40 inches	37 to 44 pounds
6 years	41 inches	42 to 51 pounds
7 years	43 inches	46 to 56 pounds
8 years	45 inches	52 to 63 pounds
9 years	47 inches	58 to 70 pounds
10 years	51 inches	63 to 77 pounds
11 years	52 inches	71 to 87 pounds
12 years	60-63 inches	86 to 116 pounds

Height and Weight Chart

Height and Weight Chart for Boys

Age	Height	Weight
2 years	31 inches	26 to 31 pounds
3 years	33 inches	30 to 36 pounds
4 years	37 inches	32 to 39 pounds
5 years	40 inches	38 to 46 pounds
6 years	42 inches	42 to 51 pounds
7 years	44 inches	46 to 56 pounds
8 years	45 inches	52 to 63 pounds
9 years	49 inches	57 to 68 pounds
10 years	51 inches	63 to 77 pounds
11 years	52 inches	71 to 84 pounds
12 years	58 to 62 inches	77 to 110 pounds

- Ask yourself:
  - Is my child too heavy?
  - Is my child having a growth spurt?
  - Is my child eating the right kind of food?
  - Is my child getting enough exercise?
  - Do I need to get help for my child?

When should I get help?

- Visit a doctor or nurse if you have questions about the height and weight chart.
- You need help measuring your child's height and weight.

Heavy Kid Feelings

What is it?

Kids usually know when they are heavy. They may feel bad about being heavy. They may not feel good about the way they look. This can affect how well they do in school and how they play. It affects what friends they have, where they hang out, and if they play sports. Being heavy affects your child's body, mind, and feelings.

Did you know?

- Many heavy kids are depressed. This means being sad, angry, or unhappy for a long time.

- No one knows if being sad, angry, or unhappy causes a kid to be heavy. It might. Or, being heavy might cause a kid to be sad, angry, or unhappy.

- No one knows of one thing that is the cause of a kid being heavy.

- The best thing to do is to work with your child to help them have a healthy weight.

- Sometimes kids eat for comfort. A crying 2 year old may stop crying when given a cookie. An older child may eat when they feel bad or unhappy.

- Many heavy kids get teased by other kids. This hurts a heavy kid's feelings. Your heavy child will feel left out. Your heavy child may not feel liked. Your heavy child may have trouble making friends.

- Many heavy kids like to eat what they want. This may be food that is not good for them. They may get mad if their parents try to change this. They may argue if their parents try to get them to eat better and exercise.

What can I do?

- Eat the right kinds of food.

- Exercise even if it is just to take a walk. Try to get your heavy child to walk when you walk.

Walk with me to the park!

- Do not allow teasing in your home. Do not allow making fun of your heavy child in your home. Your home should be a place where everyone feels loved and safe.

- Stop teasing. Be firm but nice. You can say things like:

  - I think that hurt Billy's feelings. Please do not make fun of the way people look.

  - Every person looks different. It is not polite to tease people about their size or shape.

  - Don't tease Maria about the way she looks. Let's talk about it. Teasing is not a nice thing to do.

Heavy Kid Feelings

- Try to get your heavy child to talk about being teased. Here is an example of a talk between a child, Brian, and his dad:

  Brian: I really hate baseball. I'm never going to play again.

  Dad: I thought you loved to play baseball.

  Brian: I do, but I don't like the kids on the team.

  Dad: What happened? You used to like the team.

  Brian: Well, someone called me fat and all the kids made fun of me.

  Dad: How did that make you feel?

  Brian: Really sad. I wanted to cry, but I didn't. I felt awful.

  Dad: You felt so bad you didn't want to play baseball anymore.

  Brian: That's right. But I finished the game, and I hit a home run in the last inning. We won the game.

  Dad: You seem like you really like playing baseball.

  Brian: I do, but I hate being teased.

  Dad: It really hurts when kids tease you.

  Brian: Yes, it does. I think I'm going to tell the kids not to tease me and talk to them about it.

  Dad: That sounds like a good idea.

  Brian: Some kids never tease me. I really like them. I think I will hang out with them more.

  Dad: That sounds like a really good plan. Let me know if I can help you.

- The dad in the above talk tried to let his son talk about himself and his feelings. The dad only stated his son's feelings. He let Brian make his own choice about what to do. Brian came up with a very good plan.

- Work with your heavy child to think of a way to handle teasing. Here are things your kid can do:

  - Do not show that being teased bothers you.

  - Talk in a calm way to the kids who tease. Tell them that it hurts when they tease. Ask them to stop.

  - Play with kids who do not tease.

  - Walk away.

  - Pretend you didn't hear their teasing.

  - Breathe slow and deep.

  - Count to 100. This will help them to not respond to the kid who is teasing.

  - Talk to parents of the kids who tease your heavy kid. Talk about things they can tell their kids about the pain that teasing causes a kid. The parents can tell their kids not to tease and that all kids have feelings.

When should I get help?

- Your heavy child is being teased at school. Visit your child's teacher or a counselor at school. Talk about what can be done to stop the teasing.

- Your child seems depressed.
  Visit your doctor or nurse.

Family Feelings

What is it?

Parents, brothers, and sisters have feelings about a heavy kid. They may be ashamed of a heavy kid. They may not want to be seen with a heavy kid. They may tease your heavy child. They may not ask your heavy child to play or do things with them. They may want a heavy child to lose weight. They may want to help your heavy child. But they may not know how to help.

Did you know?

- Your family may not treat your heavy child the same as other children in your family.

- Everyone in the family needs to respect your heavy child.

- Everyone in the family needs to work at helping the family and the heavy child eat good, healthy foods, play, sleep well, go to school, and have hobbies.

- There are a lot of stories about why kids are heavy. Some are true. Many are not true.

- Some families think it's OK to be heavy. They do not think it hurts their health.

- It may be hard for a child to lose weight when mom and dad are heavy.

- Mom and dad may feel bad about how they look. They may make their child feel the same way. This does not help.

- Everyone living in the home needs to help your heavy child lose weight.

- Home should be a safe place, not a place where your heavy child is unhappy. Do not allow family to tease your heavy child. Do not allow family to make fun of your heavy child.

- It is hard for a heavy child to feel good when their sisters and brothers are thin. The heavy child may be jealous of other family members.

- The heavy child may get extra attention from the parents. Thin sisters and brothers may be jealous of your heavy child.

- Family problems may be hard to solve. They affect everyone in the home.

What can I do?

- Give lots of attention to your children.

- Hugs and kisses are a good way to show how much you care for your heavy child.

- Do not use candy, sweets or food to show love and attention. Read the chapter, "Food as Reward" on page 136.

- Work together as a family to live in a healthy way. Eat meals together. Exercise together. Take the whole family for a walk.

- Do not use names such as "fatso" or "gordo" or other bad names.

- Say good things about all your children.

- Help your heavy child see good things about themselves. Say things like "Your hair looks great today." Or "I heard you did well in singing class."

- Help your heavy child meet other kids who feel OK about body size.

- Help your heavy child meet other kids who have a good attitude.

- Help your heavy child invite friends over to your home. Plan fun things to do. Play a sport. Ride a bike. Take a walk. This will help your child to be healthy.

- Don't have your child and friends just sit and watch TV. Too much sitting may make your child heavy. They may just sit and eat bad snacks. Limit TV, computer and video game time to about 1 hour per day. It is better for all kids to be active.

When should I get help?

- Your family is not helpful.

- You family will not help your heavy child.

- Your family does not work together to help your heavy child. See the chapter, "Calling for Help," on page 148.

Diet

What is it?

Some people go on a special diet to lose weight. They do things like eat less food or they do not eat any fat or carbs. These diets are called "fad diets," because everyone does them. These diets don't work. They are not healthy. You usually gain back more weight than you lose. Kids who make smart food choices and exercise usually don't need to be on a diet.

Did you know?

- A diet is what you eat and the food choices you make.
- Being on a diet means you are careful about your food choices. You are careful about how much you eat.
- Very few kids need to be on a special diet because of their weight.
- A doctor can tell you if your heavy child needs to be on a special diet.
- Kids who exercise and eat the right kind of food in the right amounts usually do not need to go on a special diet.
- Change bad eating habits into good habits. Exercise and eat well. This may be all a heavy kid needs until he grows more.

- As kids grow, their bodies need good food to be healthy. They need vitamins and minerals to help their bones and muscles grow. Read the chapter "Healthy Eating" to know what kinds of food to give your child.

- Some kids go on a fad diet because they are not happy with their bodies. Talk to your child about how he or she feels about their body.

- Some kids become upset about their weight. They try bad things. Sometimes they make themselves throw up. Sometimes they take diet pills. Read the chapters in this book, "Anorexia and Bulimia" and "Diet Pills." Talk to your doctor right away if your child is trying to lose weight this way.

- Don't call it a "diet" when your family starts to follow the eating and exercise plan in this book. Tell your family you are all going to change to a "healthy lifestyle."

What can I do?

- Talk to your child's doctor.
  - Show the doctor this book.
  - Make a plan for what your family will eat.
  - Make a plan for your child to exercise.
  - Write down what the doctor tells you.
  - Be sure to ask questions when you do not understand.
- Talk to your child about healthy food choices and bad food choices.

- Let your children know you love them.

- Let your children know that you want them to be healthy.

- Help your children make healthy food choices.

- Read this book with your children to learn healthy foods that kids should eat.

- Be a good role model. Don't tell your children to eat veggies while you eat pizza. This sends the wrong message. When your children see you eat healthy food, they will eat healthy food.

When should I get help?

- Your child is heavy.

- You are not sure how to help your child.

- You find out your child is using diet pills. Visit a doctor or nurse.

- Your child tries to throw up after meals. Talk to a doctor or nurse.

- Your child is losing or gaining a lot of weight. Talk to a doctor or nurse right away.

Healthy Eating

What is it?

Read this book to learn which foods are healthy to eat. This will help you to make better choices for you and your children. Good choices will give your children a better chance to be healthy.

Did you know?

- You can learn which foods are healthy by reading the chapter "Healthy Food" on page 30 of this book.
- Learn how to read the Nutrition Facts labels on the foods you buy. Read the chapter "Nutrition Facts Label" on page 75 of this book.
- You will make better food choices when you know which foods to buy and eat.
- You will make healthy food choices when you know how to read a Nutrition Facts label.
- You will buy foods that are better for your family's health when you know what to look for on the Nutrition Facts label. For example, look at the label of many kinds of breakfast cereal. Choose the one that has less fat and sugar, and more fiber.

What can I do?

- Teach your child how to make good food choices. Learn this together with your child. Your child may use a computer to learn about healthy food choices.

- Get rid of all the junk food in the house. Throw it away and do not buy any more.

- Make a game about healthy foods. Ask each other questions and see who knows the answer.

  - You could ask, "Which of these 3 foods is the best choice for a snack? An apple, a bag of potato chips, or a slice of white bread?" The answer is an apple, because it has less calories and fat, and more fiber. It is a fruit, which should be a big part of your food choices each day. As you learn more together, make the questions harder. Let your children make up questions for you, too.

- Look at recipes you make now and work with your child to see how you can make recipes more healthy.

  - Instead of frying chicken, steam it or boil it. Cook it on the grill. Cook it in a pan with vegetable spray. Do not fry it in oil or grease.

- If you make chili with ground beef, use ground turkey instead. It has less fat. To make chili even more healthy, add vegetables and beans. Cut up and add red and green peppers, onions, celery, and carrots.
- Use low-fat or fat-free milk, yogurt, mayo and sour cream.
- Use brown rice or whole grains like quinoa, amaranth, or barley instead of white rice.
- If you bake things like muffins, use applesauce for half the oil or shortening.
  - If the recipe calls for 2 tablespoons of oil, use 1 tablespoon of oil and 1 tablespoon of applesauce.
  - If you bake with white flour, use half white flour and half whole wheat flour.

- Look at magazines or newspapers for healthy and "light" recipes.

- Go on the computer and search for healthy recipes. Use a free computer in a library if you do not have a computer in your home. Ask your child to help you if you do not know how to use a computer.
- Talk with your doctor or nurse about how you can make healthy food for your family.

When should I get help?

- You need more ideas on how to help your family eat healthy. Look for classes on healthy eating. Check with hospitals, clinics, and schools to see if they have a class you can attend.

- You don't understand Nutrition Facts labels. Ask the grocery store manager to help you. Ask your doctor or nurse where you can get help.

Eating for
Good Health

2

Notes

_____

_____

_____

_____

_____

_____

_____

_____

_____

_____

_____

_____

_____

_____

Healthy Food

What is it?

It is important to choose healthy food for your family. It is best to choose some foods from all the food groups. This is called having a balanced diet. "Diet" is a word that means all the things you eat.

Did you know?

- There are 5 food groups you should eat from each day:
    - Vegetables (veggies)
    - Fruits
    - Grains
    - Protein
    - Dairy
- It is important to choose foods from each group every day.
- Eating foods from each food group will help your child to be healthy.
- It is important to eat the right amounts from each group. Learning how to make a healthy plate can help you.
- You can get more info about the food groups online at choosemyplate.gov.

Healthy Food

What is a healthy plate?

- A healthy plate shows the 5 food groups and how much of each group you should eat. You can use the plate to make healthy meals for you and your family.

- Think about the healthy plate each time you plan a meal for yourself or your family. It is an easy way to plan healthy meals.

- Think about the meal you want to make and how it will look on a plate. The meal will be more healthy if you follow the rules for a healthy plate.

- The size of the plate you use should be 9 inches across.

- One half of the plate should be fruits and veggies. The other half of the plate is for grains and protein.

- The place for veggies is one of the biggest parts of the plate. This is because veggies are good for you. Veggies have vitamins and lots of fiber. They help you feel full.

- The place for fruit on the plate is a little smaller. Fruit has vitamins and lots of fiber. Fruit is good for you. It will help you feel full.

- Eat more veggies than fruit. But together, veggies and fruits should fill up half of the plate.

- The place for grains is one of the biggest parts of the plate. Grains are any food made from wheat, rice, oats, cornmeal, or barley. Foods made with whole grain are more healthy because they have more fiber and vitamins in them. Try to eat more foods made with whole grains.

- The place for protein is a smaller part of the plate. Protein helps muscles and bones grow. Choose meats that are lean because they have less fat in them. Eggs, seafood, and nuts are also in this food group.

- Eat more grains than protein. But together, grains and protein should fill up half of the plate.

- Dairy is the last food group. It is not part of the plate. It is shown as a circle next to the plate. Dairy is important because it gives you calcium. This is an important mineral that grows healthy bones and teeth. Milk is one way to get calcium. You can also get it from cheese, yogurt and ice cream. These foods are also part of the milk food group. Choose milk, cheese, yogurt and ice cream that is low in fat. Choose ice cream less often.

What are some foods that make up a healthy plate?

- The healthy plate is an easy way to plan meals. Knowing what foods to use and how much to eat will help you plan meals that are more healthy.

- Choose foods from each of the 5 food groups. Use the healthy plate to know how much of each food group you should eat for a meal.

- Here is a closer look at each of the 5 food groups:

Vegetables (Veggies)

There are many different kinds of veggies. Some are <u>more healthy</u> than others. Here are some good veggies to eat:

- Cucumbers
- Spinach
- Vegetable juice
- Sweet potatoes
- Carrots
- Peppers
- Broccoli
- Tomatoes
- Zucchini and other kinds of squash

Some veggies have more starch and sugar in them. These kinds of veggies are not as healthy and you should eat less of these:

- Potatoes
- Corn
- Peas
- Veggies have vitamins and lots of fiber. They are good for you. They help you feel full. They will help your child get to a healthy weight.

- Girls should eat 2 to 2½ cup servings of veggies each day. A <u>one cup</u> serving is 1 cup of raw or cooked veggies. Two cups of raw leafy veggies is a one cup serving.

- Boys should eat 2 to 2½ cup servings of veggies each day. A <u>one cup</u> serving is 1 cup of raw or cooked veggies. Two cups of raw leafy veggies is a one cup serving.

There are many kinds of veggies. You can get your veggies fresh, frozen, or from a can. Try to eat different kinds of veggies. Eat different colors of veggies. Eat dark, leafy veggies like spinach or broccoli. Eat orange and yellow veggies like carrots, sweet potatoes, peppers, and squash.

The place for veggies is one of the biggest parts of the healthy plate. When making meals, be sure to serve lots of healthy veggies.

Fruit

- Here are some healthy fruits to eat:
  - Apples
  - Berries
  - Oranges
  - Pears
  - Melon
  - Peaches
  - Raisins

- Fruit has vitamins and lots of fiber. Fruit is good for you. It will help you feel full. Fruit will help your child get to a healthy weight.

- Girls should eat 1½ cups of fruit each day. This is about 1 large apple or grapefruit, 12 strawberries, or 1½ large peaches or oranges.

- Boys should eat 1½ cups to 2 cups of fruit each day. This is about 1½ large apples or grapefruits, 16 strawberries, or 2 large peaches or oranges.

- Fresh fruits are good for your child to eat. Get fresh fruit if you can. Look for fruits that are on sale. Buy frozen or fruit in a can when you can't get fresh fruits. You can also get dried fruit like raisins. Don't eat a lot at one time. Raisins have a lot of sugar in them.

- Look for canned fruit packed in 100% fruit juice or water. 100% juice has less sugar in it than other juices.

- Stay away from fruit packed in heavy syrup. Heavy syrup has a lot of sugar. Fruit-flavored drinks or chewy fruit rolls do not have much real fruit in them.

- Add fruit to each meal. Fruits and veggies make up half of a healthy plate.

Grains

- Grains are any food made from wheat, rice, oats, cornmeal, or barley. Here are some examples:
  - Bread
  - Tortillas
  - Pasta

- Rice
- Grits
- Breakfast cereal
- Oatmeal
- Popcorn

Girls should eat 5 or 6 one-ounce servings of grains each day. A one-ounce serving is 1 slice of bread, 1 cup of breakfast cereal, or ½ cup of cooked pasta, rice, or oatmeal.

Boys should eat 6 or 7 one-ounce servings of grains each day. A one-ounce serving is 1 slice of bread, 1 cup of breakfast cereal, or ½ cup of cooked pasta, rice, or oatmeal.

There are two kinds of grains: refined grain and whole grain. Refined means part of the grain was taken out when the food was made. White bread and white rice are examples of foods made with refined grain. Foods made with whole grain use all of the grain. These foods are more healthy because they have more fiber and vitamins in them. Try to eat more foods made with whole grains.

Look for foods that say "whole" with the name of the grain. Whole wheat, whole-grain corn, brown rice, oatmeal, and whole oats are whole-grain foods. Be careful: just because bread or tortillas are brown does not mean they are whole grain.

Look for grains that have fiber in them. Read the Nutrition Facts label. Avoid grains that have 1 gram of fiber or less.

Protein

Meats, beans, eggs, seafood, and nuts are foods that give you protein. Here are more examples from this food group:

- Lean meat
- Chicken
- Turkey
- Fish
- Seafood
- Eggs
- Beans
- Nuts
- Seeds

- Girls older than 8 should eat 5 ounces of protein each day. Each of these is a one ounce portion, so you could choose 5 of these each day: 1 ounce of meat or fish, 1 egg, 1 tablespoon of peanut butter, 2 tablespoons of hummus, ¼ cup beans, or 12 almonds.

- Boys older than 8 should eat 5 or 6 ounces of protein each day. Each of these is a one ounce portion, so you could choose 5 or 6 of these each day: 1 ounce of meat or fish, 1 egg, 1 tablespoon of peanut butter, 2 tablespoons of hummus, ¼ cup beans, or 12 almonds.

- Foods in this group give you protein. Protein helps muscles and bones grow.

- Beans have a lot of fiber. Try to add them to your meals more often. Do not cook beans in lard. This adds bad fats.

- Choose meats that say "lean" because they have less fat. For beef, choose cuts such as roasts or round steak.

- For ground beef, look on the label for "extra lean" or "90% lean." For pork, choose roasts or tenderloin. Cut away fat you can see on chicken or turkey.

- Cook chicken without the skin.

- Add protein to each meal. Protein, together with grains, make up half of a healthy plate.

Dairy

- Dairy is important because it gives you calcium. Here are examples of foods in this group:

  - Milk
  - Cheese
  - Yogurt
  - Ice cream or frozen yogurt (choose low-fat or non-fat). Do not eat more than 2 times a week.

- Girls older than 8 should eat or drink 3 cups of milk group foods each day. This could be 1 cup of milk, a small yogurt pack, and 3 slices of cheese.

- Boys older than 8 should eat or drink 3 cups of milk group foods each day. This could be 1 cup of milk, a small yogurt pack, and 3 slices of cheese.

- Choose milk, cheese, or yogurt that says low-fat or non-fat. It may also say 2% or 1% on it. This is a good choice.

- Put low-fat or non-fat yogurt and fruit in a blender to make a healthy "smoothie." Frozen fruit is a good choice for this.

- Don't use chocolate or strawberry flavored milk. They have a lot of sugar. Only have ice cream once in a while as a special treat. Do not buy it and keep it at home.

- Low-fat milk, cheese or yogurt is part of a healthy meal.

What about oils and fats?

- You need some fat and oil in your diet. There are good fats and bad fats.

- **Here are some examples of oils and fats:**
  - Butter
  - Olive oil
  - Flaxseed oil
  - Vegetable oil
  - Mayonnaise
  - Salad dressings

- Girls and boys older than 8 should have no more than 5 teaspoons of oils each day.

- Your child will get the fat and oil they need from other foods they eat, such as nuts and seeds, avocado, fish, and salad dressing.

- Stay away from fried foods. These have a lot of bad fats.

- Use only small amounts of butter or margarine. Margarine is better to use than butter. Look for margarine that has no trans fat.

- Use oil made from vegetables like olive, canola, and safflower.

- Good fats are poly fats (polyunsaturated) and mono fats (monounsaturated). Bad fats are trans fats and saturated fats, like lard.

What can I do?

- Learn about the 5 food groups with your children.

- Read the chapter in this book, "How Much Food to Eat," on page 72. Look at the chart on page 73. Know how to tell how much is in a single serving. Make sure your child knows how much is in a single serving.

- Tell your children why some foods are better for them.

- Choose different foods from each group. Choose lots of different colored veggies. Let children help choose foods at the store. Talk to them about their choices.

- Help your children make food choices that are good for their health.

- Set limits. Some foods are better for you than others. This does not mean there are foods you should never eat. One scoop of ice cream once in a while is OK. Two scoops of ice cream every day is not OK.

When should I get help?

- You are not sure which foods your child should eat.
- You do not know how much food your child should eat each day.
- Your child gains more than 2 pounds a week.
- Your child loses more than 2 pounds a week.
- Here is a guide for how much is in each serving. You can measure each serving or use this guide to help you.

A single serving of this food...	...is about the same size as a...
1 slice whole-grain bread	CD case
1 cup of pasta or rice	Tennis ball
1 medium potato	Computer mouse
2 tablespoons peanut butter	Golf ball
3 ounces cooked lean meat	Deck of cards
3 ounces fish	Cell phone
1 teaspoon of butter	1 dice
1 teaspoon mayo or dip	Thumb tip
1 cup fruit or veggies	Baseball
1 ounce of nuts	Ping-pong ball

Nutrients

What is it?

- Nutrients are in food. People need nutrients to grow, live, and stay healthy.

Did you know?

- Foods are made up of many kinds of nutrients.

- The Nutrition Facts is a label on food that you buy at the store. Read the chapter "Nutrition Facts Label" on page 75.

- The Nutrition Facts label will tell you the nutrients that are in food.

Nutrition Facts		
Serving Size 1 cup (228g)		
Servings Per Container 2		
Amount Per Serving		
Calories 250	Calories from Fat 110	
		% Daily Value*
Total Fat 12g		18%
Saturated Fat 3g		15%
Trans Fat 1.5g		
Cholesterol 30mg		10%
Sodium 470mg		20%
Total Carbohydrate 31g		10%
Dietary Fiber 0g		0%
Sugars 5g		
Protein 5g		
Vitamin A		4%
Vitamin C		2%
Calcium		20%
Iron		4%

* Percent Daily Values are based on a 2,000 calorie diet. Your Daily Values may be higher or lower depending on your calorie needs:

	Calories:	2,000	2,500
Total Fat	Less than	65g	80g
Sat Fat	Less than	20g	25g
Cholesterol	Less than	300mg	300mg
Sodium	Less than	2,400mg	2,400mg
Total Carbohydrate		300g	375g
Dietary Fiber		25g	30g

Calories

- A calorie tells how much energy it will take to use up food that has been eaten.

  - When you eat more calories than your body uses, your body will store the extra calories as fat.

  - Your body burns up calories when you exercise.

  - Some foods have calories but do not have nutrients. Soft drinks, candy, and sugary foods have a lot of calories and little nutrients. These are called "empty calorie foods."

- Some foods are low in calories and give your body many good things. Veggies and fruits are low in calories and high in nutrients.
- Ask your doctor or nurse how many calories your heavy child should eat each day.
  - Use the Nutrition Facts label to see how many calories are in a serving.
  - Be sure you read and know how much food or drink is in one serving.
  - Add the calories from each serving to know how many calories you and your child eat at each meal.
  - Add the calories from each meal to know how many calories you and your child eat in a day.

Fat
- Fat is a nutrient.
- People need some fat to stay healthy.
- Fat in food is listed on the Nutrition Facts food label.
  - Good fats that help the body are called mono fats (monounsaturated) and poly fats (polyunsaturated).
  - Foods with these fats are:
    - Fish like salmon, trout, and herring
    - Nuts like almonds, peanuts, and walnuts, and spreads made from nuts, like peanut butter and almond butter
    Do not let your children eat any nuts if they have nut allergies.

- ◆ Seeds like sunflower seeds, pumpkin seeds
- ◆ Avocados
- ■ "Saturated fats" cause people to be heavy. Stay away from foods with saturated fats.
- ■ Foods with saturated fats are:
  - ◆ Meat with fat you can see, like steak or hamburger; gravy made from any meat or poultry; sausage; and lunch meats like salami and bologna
  - ◆ Dairy products like ice cream, whole milk, and cheese that are <u>not</u> low-fat, skim, or fat-free
  - ◆ Fried foods like French fries, fried chicken, fried fish, and donuts
- ■ Never eat foods with trans fats. Foods with trans fats are:
  - ◆ Some kinds of margarine, shortening, and butter (read the Nutrition Facts label)
  - ◆ Fried foods at fast food restaurants, like French fries, fried chicken, and fried apple pie
  - ◆ Donuts, cookies, and cakes from the market
  - ◆ Any foods that say "shortening" or "hydrogenated" in the ingredients list

Protein

- Protein is a nutrient.
- Eating protein helps make us feel full.
- Some protein has a lot of bad fats. A steak or hamburger has a lot of protein but also has a lot of saturated fat.

- Some foods have a lot of protein with almost no bad fat:
  - Lean meats:
    - Chicken with the skin and fat cut off
    - Beef with no fat you can see
    - Turkey white meat
  - Fish. Salmon, trout, mackerel, albacore tuna, cod, halibut, herring
  - Beans. Pinto, black, navy, garbanzo (chick peas), kidney, black-eyed peas, lentils
  - Eggs. Cook with a cooking spray. Serve eggs poached or boiled. You can hard boil an egg and put it in your child's lunch. Buy egg whites in a carton. These have no fat and less calories than whole eggs
  - Nuts
    Do not let your children eat any nuts if they have nut allergies.

Carbs

- Carbohydrates are one source of energy your body uses. They are also called "carbs."
- Fruits, vegetables, grains, sugar, and fiber are kinds of carbs.
- Most carbs turn into sugars in your body. Fiber does not turn into sugar.
- Some carbs take much longer to turn into sugar in your body. Eat these kinds of carbs:
  - Whole-grain pasta
  - Brown rice
  - Whole-grain breads
  - Veggies

- Fruits
- Corn tortillas
- Seeds
- Beans
- Bran

- Other carbs turn into sugar very quickly in your body. Eat very little or none of these carbs:
  - Sugar
  - White bread
  - White flour tortillas
  - Fruit juice
  - Candy
  - White rice
  - Potatoes
  - Corn

What can I do?

- Make healthy choices about food.
- Use the Nutrition Facts label to find out about the nutrients in a food.
- Choose foods that are lower in calories, fat, sugar, and salt (sodium).
- Choose olive oil or canola oil in place of lard, meat fats, or butter.
- Use only a small amount of oil when you cook.

When should I get help?

- You do not understand the Nutrition Facts label.
- You do not know which proteins, carbs, or fats your child should eat.
- You are not sure if your child is getting enough vitamins and minerals. Visit your doctor or nurse, or ask your pharmacist at the drugstore.

Vitamins

What is it?

- Vitamins (**vie**-tuh-mins) are in the food we eat. Our bodies need vitamins for growth. Vitamins help our bodies stay healthy.

Did you know?

- Our bodies cannot make vitamins. We must get them from food.
- We use vitamins A, B, C, D, E, and K.
- Vitamin A helps with good eyesight, healthy hair and skin.
- Get Vitamin A from foods like these:
  - Milk
  - Orange or yellow fruits and veggies like:
    - Cantaloupe
    - Apricots
    - Squash
    - Carrots
    - Sweet potatoes
  - Dark green vegetables like:
    - Spinach
    - Broccoli
    - Collard greens
    - Kale

Vitamins

- Vitamin B helps your body use the energy from food. It also helps your blood.
- Get vitamin B from foods like these:
  - Whole grains
  - Lean meat, chicken, turkey
  - Fish
  - Eggs
  - Low-fat milk
  - Yogurt
  - Dark green veggies like spinach, collard greens, kale
  - Beans
  - Peas

- Vitamin C helps with healthy teeth, gums, and blood vessels.
- Get vitamin C from foods like these fruits and veggies:
  - Oranges
  - Kiwi
  - Strawberries
  - Pineapple
  - Cantaloupe
  - Green and red peppers
  - Broccoli
  - Cauliflower
  - Brussels sprouts

- Vitamin D helps with healthy bones and teeth. It helps your body use minerals like calcium.
- Get vitamin D from foods like these:
  - Low-fat milk
  - Eggs
  - Fish
  - Some cereals
  - Sunshine for a short time helps your body to use vitamin D. You should always wear sunscreen when out in the sun for a long time.
- Vitamin E helps you keep healthy eyes, skin, blood, and lungs.
- Get Vitamin E from foods like these:
  - Nuts
  - Peanut butter
  - Avocado
  - Dark green vegetables like spinach, collard greens, kale
  - Whole grains
  - Egg yolks
- Vitamin K helps your blood.
- Get Vitamin K from foods like these:
  - Milk
  - Yogurt
  - Eggs

Vitamins

- Dark green, leafy vegetables like spinach, collard greens, and kale
- Meats

What can I do?

- Eat foods from all the food groups.
- Give your heavy child a vitamin pill if your doctor tells you to. Vitamins do not make your child heavy or hungry.

When should I get help?

- You do not know if your child needs to take vitamin pills.
- You are not sure if your child is eating all the right foods.

Food Shopping

What is it?

Going to the store to buy healthy food. Keep healthy food in your home. This will make it easy for your family and your heavy child to eat the right food.

Did you know?

- When you buy groceries and cook meals at home it costs less to eat. When you buy fast food or eat out all the time it will cost more.
- Foods that cost less are usually on high and low shelves in the middle aisles.
- The best choices in a grocery store are usually around the outside walls, and in the cold section. This is where you will find fruits and veggies, fresh foods like milk and cheese, and meats and fish.

What can I do?

- Take your children with you to the store.
- Let your children help choose healthy food to buy.
- Eat before you shop. If you are hungry when you shop you will buy things that may not be healthy for you. You may buy foods you want to eat right away.
- Make a list before going to the store. This way you will buy things that are healthy and good for you.

- Use coupons. They let you buy food for less money. Don't use coupons to buy unhealthy food.

- Buy foods that are on sale. This way you can spend a little more on fresh foods that are good for you.

- Look for store brands. They cost less and often taste the same.

- Plan your meals for the week. Then make your grocery list. Think about what you want to put in your child's lunch bag. Plan what things you will need to make the meals. Be sure to include lots of veggies, whole grains, fruits, and some meat, fish and beans. Read the chapter "Healthy Eating" on page 24.

- When you buy meat or fish, choose cuts that have less fat. Remove the skin from chicken when you get home. Chicken without the skin costs more than buying a whole chicken and cutting off the skin at home.

- Buy fresh fish that does not have a "fishy" smell. Ask if fish is fresh when you buy fish or meat at the butcher counter. It should not be slimy or sticky. If you buy fish or meat that is in a package, check the label for the date when it can no longer be sold. Use it on or before this date.

Food Shopping

- Look for "whole grain" in the ingredients list. Read the labels on bread, pasta, crackers, and tortillas. Food that is whole grain has more fiber. Fiber helps food move slower through your body. You will feel full longer.

- Go to the market a few times a week to buy fresh fruit and veggies. Get only the amount your family will eat until you shop again.

- Look for fruit that is firm and not too ripe. Fruit is best for you when it is firm and not too soft. Fruits like bananas or pears should not have a lot of brown or black spots on them.

- Look closely at fresh fruit. Mold can form on some fresh fruits like berries.

- Buy different kinds of fruit. Some fruit last longer than others. Apples, grapefruit, oranges, and grapes stay fresh for a long time. Bananas, pears, and berries have to be eaten in a few days.

- Most fresh foods will have a date on the package. Eat these foods before this date.

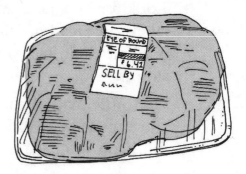

- Some foods have a date that says "Packed on." This is the day they were put into the bag or box. This is not the date they go bad. Ask the person who works at the store how long this food will last.

- Keep some frozen and canned fruits and veggies in your home. If you cannot get to the store, you will still have fruits and veggies to eat. Rinse canned veggies before cooking or eating.

- Choose veggies with many different colors:
  - Dark green, leafy veggies like spinach and kale
  - Orange veggies like carrots, peppers, and squash
  - Red veggies like tomatoes and peppers

When should I get help?

- You are not sure what to buy at a grocery store.
- You need help making good food choices.

Paying for Healthy Food

What is it?

Shopping for fresh and healthy food can cost more money. It is worth the extra cost. There are ways you can buy healthy food so it does not cost too much.

Did you know?

- You may be able to get help getting healthy food from a program called WIC (Women, Infants, Children). There are other programs to help you buy food if you do not make a lot of money. Ask your doctor or nurse to refer you to someone who can help you apply for these programs.

- Some healthy food can be frozen. Look for sales and buy extra of these foods when they cost less. You may spend more now. You will have food later. You will save money.

- Your food will stay healthy if you follow these rules when you freeze your food:

  - Use plastic bags that say "freezer" on the box. These will help keep your food good.

  - Squeeze all the air out of the bags before you seal food in them. If you don't, your food will get freezer burn and won't taste good.

- For meat, fish, or poultry, you can use freezer paper instead of plastic bags. Wrap the food so it is against the shiny side of the paper.

- You can also use plastic wrap, but use two layers to protect your food.

- Wash and dry your meat, fish, poultry, fruits, and veggies before you freeze them. Pat them dry with a paper towel. Be sure they are dry. If they are not dry, ice will form on the food and spoil it.

- Store your food in amounts that you will use for one meal. Use one package at each meal.

- Write on the outside of the package what is inside, and the date that you froze it. Then you will know what it is and if it is still good.

- Defrost frozen food by putting it in the fridge overnight. Do not leave frozen food out on the counter overnight to thaw. It will get germs and can make you sick.

- Don't put too much frozen food in your freezer. Allow some space in your freezer so the cold air can move around your foods.

- Here are some healthy foods you can buy on sale and freeze.

  - Whole-grain bread will keep for 2 months.

  - Lean meat, fish, and poultry (like lean chicken or turkey) will keep for 3 months.

  - Fresh veggies like:

    - Asparagus

- Green beans
- Broccoli
- Carrots
- Mushrooms
- Onions
- Sweet peppers (red, green, or yellow)
- Spinach
- Squash or zucchini can be frozen. But you must blanch them first.

> - To blanch, wash the veggie well.
> - Boil in water for 3 minutes or until tender.
> - Put them right away in very cold water for 5 minutes to stop them from cooking.

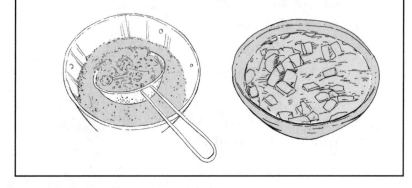

- Cut up bigger veggies before freezing. Use these veggies in recipes you cook. They are not as good to eat plain and raw after they have been frozen.
- Frozen veggies will last about 8 months.
- Some fresh fruits may be frozen.

- Better choices are berries, peaches, and bananas.
- Wash these first, and dry.
- Peel bananas before freezing.
- Peel and cut up peaches first. Throw out the pit.
- Use frozen fruit in smoothies or on cereal.
- Fruit will be soft and a little mushy when you defrost them.
- Fruit will keep for 8 months.

What can I do?

- Choose the store brand. Store brands are also called "generics." They are often made just the same as the name brands.
- Check the label of the store brand to see if it has the same calories, fat, or salt as the name brand.

- Some stores let you buy food in bulk.
  - Put as much as you want to buy in a bag.
  - Pay for it by the pound.

- Some foods that you can buy in bulk are nuts, whole-grain flour, cereals, rice, and pasta.

- This costs less than buying food in a box.

- Use coupons. The money you save will help you pay for fresh and healthy foods. Find coupons in newspapers, your mail, at your store, or on your computer.

- See if you have a farmer's market near your home. You can get fresh fruits and veggies that are grown locally. Many times they cost less and are fresher than what you buy at the grocery store.

- If you can get to more than one store easily, buy the foods that cost less from each of those stores. You may pay less for fruits and veggies at a store that only sells that.

- Watch for sales.
  - Buy what is on sale.
  - Buy what you need plus a little extra.
  - Freeze the extra food.
  - Buy only what you can use, freeze, or keep for awhile.

- Some foods are sold the day before they go bad at a lower price. Foods like meat, poultry, fish, or bread. Buy these if you know you can use them right away.

- Some foods are sold in "family packs."

  - Look for this kind of package.

  - Check the price per pound. Make sure it is lower than the price per pound of the smaller package.

  - Ask family or friends if they want to share the "family pack" and split the cost.

  - Freeze what you cannot use for one meal.

When should I get help?

- You do not think you can afford to buy healthy food.

- You are not sure how to freeze some kinds of food.

- You are not able to buy enough food for your family.

Mealtime

3

Notes

61

Cook Healthy

What is it?

Healthy cooking is a way to cook that lowers the fat and calories in meals. Healthy cooking keeps the nutrients and vitamins in the food. The food you serve will be good for your heavy child. It will be good for your whole family.

Did you know?

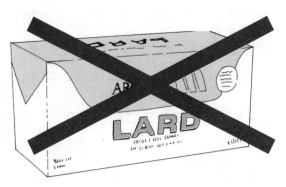

- Some ways to cook add too much fat.

- Cooking foods in oil, fat, shortening, or lard like Crisco or bacon drippings adds fat to the food.

- Cooking with fat is not a good way to cook your food. Do not deep fry your food. This will add a lot of fat. Too much fat is not good for your family's health.

- You can change some things in recipes so your food is healthy and still tastes good.

- Do not dip your food in batter or flour to cook it. This will add fat and calories.

- Only use enough oil to coat a pan. Use cooking spray, like Pam. Or use broth to cook instead of oil. Using broth for a stir fry will add flavor and less fat. Choose broth that says "lower sodium."

- You can cook on a grill. This is a good way to cook meats because it lets the fat drain away from the food. Do not cook meat until it is black and burned. Black or burned meat is not healthy. Cook on a lower heat so it does not burn.

- Make sure your meat is cooked well. Cut open a piece to make sure it is cooked all the way through.

- You can cook veggies and fish on the grill. Use a basket made for a grill. Before you start the grill you can cover the grill with tin foil and poke holes in it.

- You can cook veggies in the microwave. You can steam or boil veggies in water. Or you can cover the grill with tin foil and poke holes in it. Do this before you light the grill.

- Eat less red meat. Red meat is roast beef, hamburger, lamb, and steaks. Serve fish, pork, chicken, or turkey, too. Add beans for protein. When you serve red meat, choose lean meats. Trim away fat that you can see.

- Meats like bacon and ham, hot dogs, and lunch meats like bologna and salami have a lot of salt and fat. Do not eat a lot of these meats.

- Serve water, low-fat milk, or non-fat milk with meals. Do not serve soda pop with meals.

- Try to have meals with no meat sometimes. Serve beans or tofu for protein.

Cook Healthy

What can I do?

- Do not serve food family style with all foods on big plates or in bowls at the table. Put food on each person's plate and then put the plate on the table. This way you can make sure your child gets the right amount of each food. Let your kids help you do this.

- Put away leftovers in the fridge. Serve them for lunch or dinner the next day.

- Before you cook meat or chicken, cut off the fat.

- Use cooking spray like Pam in place of fat or oil when you fry food in a pan. This will keep food from sticking to the pan. It is much healthier.

- Veggies are more healthy when they are still firm. Do not cook them until they are soft and mushy.

- Buy fresh veggies. Ask the person who works at the store to show you how to choose good fresh veggies.

- If your store does not have fresh veggies, buy canned or frozen. These are good choices, too. Rinse canned veggies before cooking or eating.

- Steam your veggies. Add a little lemon juice. Sprinkle on spices, herbs, or a little cheese and serve. Choose shredded cheeses like Parmesan or Romano.

- Add veggies whenever you can. Put them in soups or stews. Make a stir fry meal with a lot of veggies. Chop up veggies of all colors and cook them in the same pan with meat, fish, or chicken.

- Serve a salad with lunch or dinner. This will help your family to eat more veggies. It will also help to make them feel full.

- Eat slowly. This will help you and your child not to eat too much.

- Drink water with each meal.

- Use spices to make foods taste good. Try spices like garlic, pepper, oregano, or curry or fresh herbs like basil, rosemary, or cilantro.

- Buy a steamer basket to steam your foods.

- The steamer basket opens out and goes in the bottom of a pan.

  - Put about 1 inch of water in the pan.

  - Put in the steamer basket. You should not see water above the bottom of the steamer basket. If you do, pour a little bit out.

- Wait until the water boils.
- Put your food in the basket.
- Cover the pan with a lid. Don't let all the water boil away. Add a little bit of hot water if it gets too low.
- Cook until veggies are cooked but still firm, about 3-5 minutes.
- The steam from the boiling water cooks the food. The lid helps keep the steam in the pan to cook the food.
- **The steam is hot. Be careful to not burn yourself. Use a pot holder. Open the lid slowly. Open it away from your face.**
- Choose whole-grain pasta, grains, or brown rice in place of white pasta or white rice.
- Use beans to add protein to a vegetarian meal.
- Serve fruits and berries for dessert instead of cake, pie, ice cream, or other foods that have a lot of sugar. Serve with a little non-fat whipped cream or non-fat yogurt.

When should I get help?
- You need to know how to cook food without frying.
- Your family will not eat the healthy food that you cook.

Family Meals

What is it?

The family meal is when the family sits at the table and eats together. This is a time when all of the family sits down to eat. Grandma and grandpa, aunts and uncles, cousins, and friends may also be at a family meal.

Did you know?

- Kids and teens who have a meal such as dinner with the family do better at school. They are not as likely to be heavy.

- School-age kids who eat meals with the family do better at school.

- Sometimes older kids do not want to eat meals with their family. Parents should still try to get teens to eat with the family.

- Eating with the family helps everyone eat a healthy diet. Children are more likely to eat fruits and veggies at a family meal. Your children will eat what the family eats. Your children will take time to eat. Your children will eat a healthy meal.

Family Meals

- Write out a weekly dinner menu. Put it in a place where everyone can see it. Children can help cook dinner when you are busy. Have them help with dishes when the meal is done. Cleaning up is part of the family meal.

- Teens who eat with the family at dinner time use less tobacco, booze, and drugs.

- The family meal is just as important in families with one parent. If you are a single parent, have dinner with your children at least 2 or 3 times a week.

- The family meal is a time to talk to each other, support each other, and talk about the day's activities. It is a time to share ideas, thoughts, and feelings. Talk about:

  - Healthy food
  - How to make good choices
  - Why healthy food choices are good for your body and mind

- Children learn how to care for themselves when they help buy the food, cook, and clean up after eating.

- Children learn by watching adults use good manners, make healthy food choices, and choose small serving sizes.

- Children can learn to pour, scoop, serve, share, and take turns while fixing the family meal.

What can I do?

- Let your children help cook the family meal. This is a time when you can talk and listen to your children.

- Serve everyone the same healthy meal. Do not serve your child a healthy meal and everyone else food that is not healthy. Your heavy child may feel that he or she is being punished.

- Try not to serve foods that are high in sugar. A cookie or bite of cake once in awhile is OK.

- Plan to have your child eat at the table. Children under 5 may have trouble sitting for a long time at the dinner table. Plan shorter meals.

- Fix food ahead to help cut down the work at dinner time. Cook on the weekend. Cook food that you can freeze. Cook food for the week ahead.

- Turn off the TV or radio during the family meal.

- Have your family meal when all your family can be at the table. There are a lot of ways to have a family meal. Have a picnic. Eat at a restaurant. Eat together. Having the family together is the important thing.

- Make sure all the children in the family have a chance to talk and share during the family meal. Do not let one child do all the talking.

- Talk to your children during the family meal. Things to talk about are:
  - What happened during the day
  - Healthy foods
  - When is the next day's meal

- Best liked things the family does together
- Least liked things the family does together
- Plans for the weekend
- A book someone in the family is reading
- School, teachers, and homework. Find out if your children need help with their homework.

- Put family mealtimes on a calendar or on the fridge so everyone knows the time of the family meal. Try to have meals at the same time each night. Let the family know the time of dinner.

- Try to get all the children to eat at the same time.

- Make the family meal fun by having fun foods. For dinner, build your own tacos or burritos. For breakfast, cut toast or pancakes into fun shapes with cookie cutters. Make fun faces on pancakes with fruit and low-fat whipped cream.

- Talk to your children. Listen to your children as they tell you about their day. Try not to get mad or argue during the family meal.

- Keep meals simple and easy.

- Have all family members be a part of having the family meal. Family members can buy food, cook, and clean up after the meal.

- Turn off the TV, radio, or music during the family meal. Make the family meal a time for talking to each other.

- Do not use food as a reward for doing something good.

- Children should eat only if they are hungry. Children should not be told to "finish their plate."

- Have your children eat some food from each food group.

- The family meal is a good time to give children new and healthy foods. Talk about the new foods and why they are healthy.

- Still have a family meal if only 1 parent or 1 or 2 children can be home at dinner time.

When should I get help?

- Your family will not eat together.
- Family is too busy to eat together.
- There are family fights during mealtime.
- Sports games take place at dinner time. Talk to the coach.
- School activities or meetings take place at dinner time. Talk to your child's teacher.

How Much Food to Eat

What is it?

A portion is how much of each food you eat at one time. It may also be called a serving or a helping.

Did you know?

- Eating the right size portion helps your family eat the right amount of food each day. Your family will eat enough food. Your family will not eat too much food.

- The amount of food you eat now may not be the same as the serving size listed on the Nutrition Facts label. It may be too much to be a healthy portion.

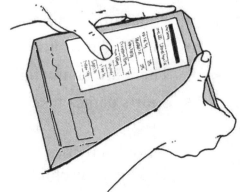

- Read the Nutrition Facts label on the box, can, or bottle to know how much is a single serving.

- For some foods, you can have more than one serving at a meal. You can eat more than one serving at a time of fruits, vegetables, and whole grains.

How Much Food to Eat

- Here's a way to make a good guess how much is a single serving. See how much would fit in the palm of your hand. Only do this for fruits, veggies, and proteins. Do not do it for carbs, fats, and sweets.

- Here is an easy guide to know about how much food is in a single serving.

A single serving of this food...	...is about the same size as a...
1 slice whole-grain bread	CD case
1 cup pasta or rice	Tennis ball
1 medium potato	Computer mouse
2 tablespoons peanut butter	Golf ball
3 ounces cooked lean meat	Deck of cards
3 ounces fish	Cell phone
1 teaspoon butter	1 dice
1 teaspoon mayo or dip	Thumb tip
1 cup fruit or veggies	Baseball
1 ounce nuts	Ping-pong ball

What can I do?

- Measure out portions first before giving them to your child. Put the food on a plate or in a bowl. Do not let kids eat food out of a bag or box. They will not know how much they are eating. This can lead to eating more than a single serving.

- When eating out, share meals. Do not get a super size meal. Cut big portions in two and ask for a "to go" box. Read the chapter "Restaurants" on page 143 for more ideas. Read the chapter "Fast Food" on page 104, too.

- Use smaller plates when you eat at home. A larger plate with small portion sizes may make children feel they are not getting enough food. A smaller plate that is filled will make children feel they have a full meal.

- If your child asks for extra portions, first offer extra fruits and veggies.

- Ask your child to help you think of other things that match portion sizes. Use things that they use every day, such as an iPod, bar of soap, stick of chewing gum, their fist, and the palm of their hand.

When should I get help?

- You are not sure how much food your child should be eating.

- Your child always says he or she is hungry after eating the right size portion.

- You do not understand food labels or portion sizes.

- Your child argues with you about how much to eat.

- Your child is hiding food to eat later.

- Your child sneaks extra food when you are not looking.

Nutrition Facts Label

What is it?

Most food that you buy in a store has a label on it called the Nutrition Facts label. It looks like the picture on this page. You can use this label to choose the right foods for your child to eat.

Did you know?

- The Nutrition Facts label will tell you about the food that is in the box, can, or package.
- Here is an example of a Nutrition Facts label.
- **Serving Size.** This tells you how much of the food to eat at one time. It is one portion. This label tells you that the serving size is one cup.
- **Servings per Container.** Tells how many servings, or portions, are inside the box, can, or package. This label tells you this container has two servings.

Nutrition Facts		
Serving Size 1 cup (228g)		
Servings Per Container 2		
Amount Per Serving		
Calories 250	Calories from Fat 110	
		% Daily Value*
Total Fat 12g		18%
Saturated Fat 3g		15%
Trans Fat 1.5g		
Cholesterol 30mg		10%
Sodium 470mg		20%
Total Carbohydrate 31g		10%
Dietary Fiber 0g		0%
Sugars 5g		
Protein 5g		
Vitamin A		4%
Vitamin C		2%
Calcium		20%
Iron		4%

* Percent Daily Values are based on a 2,000 calorie diet. Your Daily Values may be higher or lower depending on your calorie needs:

	Calories:	2,000	2,500
Total Fat	Less than	65g	80g
Sat Fat	Less than	20g	25g
Cholesterol	Less than	300mg	300mg
Sodium	Less than	2,400mg	2,400mg
Total Carbohydrate		300g	375g
Dietary Fiber		25g	30g

- **Calories.** This tells how many calories are in each serving. This is not the number of calories in the whole container. 40 is a low number of calories. 400 is a high number of calories. This label tells you that there are 250 calories in one serving.

- **Total Fat.** This tells how much fat is in each serving. Look for foods with a low number of total fat. Look for foods that have low or no saturated fats and no trans fats. If it has fat, choose foods that have mono fats (monounsaturated) and poly fats (polyunsaturated) instead. This label tells you that the food has saturated and trans fats. This label tells you there is 12g of fat in one serving. This is high for one serving. Choose foods that have 5g or less of fat per serving. Look for another similar food with lower total fat.

- **Sodium.** Sodium means salt. This tells how much salt is in each serving. Look for foods that are lower in sodium (salt). Low sodium would be 140mg or less. This label tells you that there are 470mg of sodium in one serving. This is high for one serving. Look for another food that has less sodium.

- **Total Carbohydrate.** This tells the amount of carbs, fiber, and sugar in each serving. If it has fiber, choose foods that have a high fiber number. Fiber is found only in fruits, veggies, and grains. There is no fiber in meat, fish, or dairy.

  - A high fiber food is 5g or more fiber per serving. This label tells you that there is no fiber in one serving. Try to choose foods that have at least 2 grams of fiber per serving.

- Sugar on the label is sugar found in food and added to food. Check the ingredients list for added sugars. Choose foods that are low in sugar. This label tells you that there is 5g of sugar in one serving. Try to choose foods that have 8g or less of sugar per serving.

Nutrition Facts

Serving Size 1 cup (228g)
Servings Per Container 2

Amount Per Serving

Calories 250	Calories from Fat 110

	% Daily Value*
Total Fat 12g	18%
Saturated Fat 3g	15%
Trans Fat 1.5g	
Cholesterol 30mg	10%
Sodium 470mg	20%
Total Carbohydrate 31g	10%
Dietary Fiber 0g	0%
Sugars 5g	
Protein 5g	

Vitamin A	4%
Vitamin C	2%
Calcium	20%
Iron	4%

* Percent Daily Values are based on a 2,000 calorie diet. Your Daily Values may be higher or lower depending on your calorie needs:

	Calories:	2,000	2,500
Total Fat	Less than	65g	80g
Sat Fat	Less than	20g	25g
Cholesterol	Less than	300mg	300mg
Sodium	Less than	2,400mg	2,400mg
Total Carbohydrate		300g	375g
Dietary Fiber		25g	30g

- **Protein.** This tells how much protein is in each serving. Kids need 46 to 52 grams of protein a day. Choose proteins like fish, lean chicken and turkey, and lean pork and beef. Tofu is a good source of protein. Beans, nuts, seeds, and eggs have protein, too. This label tells you that there is 5g of protein in one serving.

- **Nutrients.** This label tells you that the food contains Vitamin A, Vitamin C, calcium, and iron.

What can I do?

- Use the Nutrition Facts label when you plan meals.
- Use the Nutrition Facts label when you shop.
- Use the Nutrition Facts label when you cook.
- Use the Nutrition Facts label to know what portion of the food to serve your child.

Nutrition Facts Label

- Look at the Serving Size on the box, can, or package of food.
- Check the number of Servings per Container on the Nutrition Facts label. Make sure you and your children know how much food is in a Serving before you eat it.
  - Some containers have many servings in them. Cereal and ice cream have many servings.
  - Some containers have only one serving. A small yogurt cup has one serving.
- Use the information on the Nutrition Facts label to help you know what your child is eating for a day. The Nutrition Facts label will help you keep track of:
  - Calories
  - Fat
  - Sodium (salt)
  - Sugar
  - Fiber
  - Protein
- Read the Nutrition Facts label with your child. This will help your child learn to make good food choices.

When should I get help?

- You are not sure how to read the Nutrition Facts label.
- You are not sure how much of each of the nutrients on the label your child should have each day.
- Tell your doctor or nurse what your child eats each day. Ask if this diet is best for your child.

Food for a Heavy Child 4

_____

_____

_____

_____

_____

_____

_____

_____

_____

_____

_____

_____

Breakfast

What is it?

Breakfast is the first meal of the day. Breakfast is the most important meal of the day.

Did you know?

- Eating a healthy breakfast each day will help your child:
  - Pay attention in school
  - Do chores
  - Have more energy
  - Not feel hungry before lunch
  - Keep at a healthy weight
- Children who eat a good breakfast have less chance to be heavy.
- Children who eat a good breakfast have less chance of having diabetes.
- Some schools offer low cost or free breakfast. Check with your child's school.
- There are many good choices for breakfast:
  - Oatmeal is a good whole-grain choice. Instant oatmeal is as good as the kind you

must cook in a pan. Do not buy instant oatmeal that already has sugar in it. Be sure to read the label. Add any of these to make plain oatmeal taste better:

- ◆ Fruit like raisins, bananas, berries
- ◆ Low-fat or non-fat milk
- ◆ Cinnamon
- ◆ Granola

- Eggs. You can also buy egg whites in a carton ready to pour and cook. Egg whites have less fat and calories than whole eggs. Add veggies to scrambled eggs. A little cheese will make it taste better. Serve with whole wheat toast or in a whole wheat tortilla.

- Cereal. Do not buy cereals that have a lot of sugar. Many cereals have as much sugar as a donut or candy. Look for cereal that has 5 grams or less of sugar per serving. Choose cereal that has at least 2 grams of fiber per serving. Add fruit to cereal to make it taste good. Use low-fat or non-fat milk.

- Breakfast burrito. Scramble eggs with peppers and add beans and a little low-fat or non-fat cheese. Use a whole wheat tortilla. Do not fry the tortilla.

- Pancakes or waffles. Choose frozen waffles that have whole grains. You can heat these in the toaster. Add fruit like blueberries or strawberries to pancake batter before cooking.

- Bagel. Choose whole-grain bagels and use low-fat or non-fat cream cheese.

- Yogurt and fruit. Kids like to hold food and to dip it. Choose low-fat or non-fat yogurt to use as a dip. Use fruits with different colors, like:

  - Strawberries
  - Blueberries
  - Kiwi
  - Mango
  - Pineapple
  - Pears
  - Apples that are sliced and still have the peel on

- Try adding low-fat or non-fat granola to yogurt. This will make it crunchy and tasty. Granola is a good grain choice. Choose granola without a lot of sugar.

- Smoothie. Put fruit, plain low-fat or non-fat yogurt, low-fat or non-fat milk, and a little bit of juice in a blender. Frozen fruits work well in smoothies. Don't use citrus fruits like oranges, grapefruit or lemons in smoothies. They don't blend well in a blender. Bananas, berries, and peaches are good choices. Your child can drink this on the way to school.

- Here are some choices that are not as good. **Avoid these foods:**

  - Donuts and pastries. Donuts, cinnamon buns, toaster pastries, pan dulce, coffee cake, and other sweet breakfast breads have a lot of sugar and fat. They have almost no nutrients and a lot of calories.

  - Bacon, sausage, and chorizo have a lot of fat and salt. Choose other breakfast meats like turkey sausage or soy breakfast meats. Make these a small part of breakfast.

  - Anything cooked with a lot of oil, bacon grease, or shortening. Use a cooking spray to keep foods from sticking to the pan. Sprays have less fat than oil, grease, or shortening.

  - Whole milk. Before age 1, breast milk or formula is best. Between age 1 and 2, ask your doctor or nurse if you should give whole milk or low-fat milk. After age 2, use low-fat milk. Milk that is low in fat has the same vitamins and nutrients.

  - Frozen breakfast meals may have a lot of fat, sugar, calories, and sodium. Do not buy breakfast sandwiches, burritos, and sweetened pastries with frosting.

What can I do?

- Make breakfast a healthy meal.
- Help your child to choose foods that are healthy.

When should I get help?

- Your heavy child will not eat breakfast.

Lunch

What is it?

Lunch is the meal your child eats around 12 noon. Lunch is eaten between breakfast and dinner. During the week your child may eat lunch at school. Very young children eat lunch at home, nursery school, or preschool.

Did you know?

- Kids need to eat a healthy lunch. It is not healthy to skip lunch when trying to lose weight.
- Lunch will give your child energy until snack or dinner time.
- Lunch should be made with foods that have nutrients for good health.
- Eating healthy will cost less than quick snacks. A sandwich may cost less than snack food. A sandwich is a better choice than a candy bar or chips.
- Fruit juices and soda pop have a lot of sugar and calories. Low-fat milk or water is a better choice for kids.

What can I do?

- Shop for lunch items at the store.
- Food to buy for lunch that is healthy:
  - Whole wheat bread for sandwiches

- Peanut butter **if your child is not allergic to peanuts**. Some schools do not allow peanut butter to be brought to school.
- Fresh fruits and veggies
- Tuna fish
- Tomatoes
- Lean roast beef
- Lean turkey

- Get little kids used to healthy foods like fruits and veggies.
- Don't give kids high-calorie or high-fat foods like candy, cake, cookies, or muffins.
- Make lunches the night before so they are ready to take to school.
- Put things that need to be cool in the fridge. Use insulated lunch boxes or bags with frozen ice bags or gel packs.
- Serve healthy desserts like fresh fruits. Grapes, melon, or apple slices are better choices than candy bars or cookies.
- Take your children shopping. Let them choose some of their own healthy food. Your children can choose the fruit or veggies that they like. Children will want to eat foods that they choose.

- Add lettuce and tomato to a sandwich. This will help your child fill up on healthy food.

- Watch the portion size. Give your child only one sandwich and a healthy dessert. Don't give your child any sweet or fatty desserts.

- Do not buy lunches that you can buy "ready made" at the store. These lunches have a lot of calories and salt.

- Low-fat milk and water are good things to drink. Don't give your child chocolate milk, fruit juice, fruit drinks, sugar drinks, or soft drinks.

- Have children make lists of all the foods they like in each food group: fruits, veggies, whole grains, milk, and protein.
  - Put this list where everyone can see it.
  - Have children choose at least one food from the list each day.
  - Children will be more likely to eat foods that they choose.
  - Get excited when your kid eats a healthy lunch.

- Serve lunch about the same time each day. This helps get children used to eating at regular mealtimes.

- Don't make children clean their plate. It is OK to leave some food that has not been eaten.

- Don't use food as a way to show love.

- Don't use food to get your children to do what you want them to do.

- Give your children new and healthy things to eat. This will make eating fun.

- Make lunch from leftover food. This can be healthy and can save money.
- Many children like to dip things in their lunch. Use a little cup with a lid to keep peanut butter or low-fat ranch dressing as a dip for veggies. This makes the food fun and healthy. Do not give your child peanut butter if they are allergic to nuts.

When should I get help?

- Your heavy child does not want to eat healthy. Visit your doctor or nurse, teacher, or school counselor.
- Your thin child is not eating healthy.
- You feel your children are not eating healthy.
- Your heavy child eats all day long.
- You find out your heavy child trades healthy lunch for bad snacks at school.
- Your child argues with you about what to pack and eat for lunch.

School Lunch

What is it?

School lunch is a meal your child will eat away from home. A healthy lunch will help your child do well in school.

Did you know?

- Keeping hot foods hot and cold foods cold can be hard.

- It is important to keep hot foods hot and cold foods cold so they do not get germs that can make your child sick.

- Look for a lunch pack or box that helps keep cold foods cold and hot foods hot. Wash these out with hot, soapy water when your child brings them home.

- Cold foods such as meat, mayo, cheese, milk, and eggs must be kept at 40 degrees or cooler.

- Ask if there is a refrigerator at school where your child can put his or her lunch.

- Some schools offer low cost or free lunches. Check with your child's school.

- For cold foods, put a frozen gel pack in your child's lunch pack.

School Lunch

- A gel pack is a sealed bag with gel in it that you freeze overnight.
- The frozen gel pack will keep cold foods cold.
- Be sure to tell your child to bring it home each night.
- Put it back in the freezer at night so it's ready to use again in the morning.

- Freeze a small bottle of water or a juice box overnight. It will melt by lunch time so your child can drink the water or juice. Choose a juice that is 100% fruit juice with no added sugar.

- For hot foods, try an insulated food jar. Ask if your child can heat up food in a microwave at school. This will give you more choices for your child's lunch.

- Choose foods from each of the five basic food groups: vegetables, fruits, whole grains, milk, and protein.

- Oils are a food group too, but you only need a little each day. You get oil from other healthy foods you eat.

- Choose different foods each day if you can so your children do not get bored and trade their food for less healthy foods at school. Talk to your children and ask if they like what they had today. Sometimes kids like the same food every day. This is OK for awhile as long as the food is healthy.

- Leftovers from dinner are OK to send to school for lunch.

- Choose healthy lunch foods from each food group.

Whole Grains

- Use whole-grain bread to make sandwiches. Make sandwiches fun by using a cookie cutter to shape the sandwiches.

- Use a whole-grain mini bagel instead of bread for a sandwich.

- Put sliced lean meat and low-fat cheese in a whole wheat tortilla. Roll it up and slice it into bite-size pieces. Good lean meat choices include turkey, chicken, and lean roast beef. Add hummus or salsa.

- Use whole wheat pita bread. Pita bread has a pocket that you can put fillings into. Make a tuna salad filling. Buy canned tuna that is packed in water. Use fat-free mayo, chopped celery, and peppers. Add tomato for a healthy tuna sandwich.

- Make a healthy sandwich from peanut butter, cashew butter, or almond butter and 100% fruit spread on whole-grain bread or in a pita bread. **Do not use peanut butter, cashew butter, or almond butter if your child has a nut allergy.**

- Include some whole-grain crackers or pretzels along with low-fat cheese. This is a good choice for something crunchy and a little salty in place of potato chips.

- Mix brown rice, whole wheat pasta or couscous with chopped vegetables, like cucumbers, peppers, and tomatoes.

Veggies

- Baby carrots, celery sticks, and green beans. Include a dip such as hummus, low-fat or non-fat yogurt, or bean dip.
- Salad.
  - ◆ You can pack salad in a small plastic container with a snap-on lid.
  - ◆ Choose dark, leafy veggies like spinach or romaine lettuce.
  - ◆ Add sliced cucumbers, raw broccoli, shredded carrots, cherry tomatoes or sliced tomatoes, and other veggies or fruits your kid likes.
  - ◆ Pack dressing separately so the salad does not get soggy. Use low-fat or fat-free dressings.
  - ◆ Pack a plastic fork.
- Grate or chop up veggies into small pieces and mix them with many other foods.
- Chop up peppers, celery, and other crunchy veggies with tuna or chicken salad.

- Steam veggies like broccoli and cauliflower and put them in a blender, or just mash with a fork. You can then add these to tomato sauce to get more veggies in pasta.

- Add dark leafy lettuce, tomato slices, and thin sliced cucumbers to sandwiches.

- Vegetable soup is good on a cold day. If your child cannot heat it up at school, pack it in a thermos container in the morning. Be sure to wash the container with hot, soapy water each night.

Fruits

- Bananas. Half a banana may be enough for a small child.

- Apples, whole or sliced. For sliced apples, think about a dip such as low-fat or non-fat vanilla yogurt. Always leave the peel on. The peel has fiber and vitamins.

- Add berries to the top of yogurt. Blueberries, strawberries, blackberries and raspberries are good choices.

- Applesauce. You can buy single-serving packs. Choose ones that do not have added sugar.

- Oranges are fun to peel and eat in sections. If your child does not have much time at lunch, peel it before you put it in his or her lunch.

- Raisins are a good choice and come in boxes that fit in lunch bags.

- Sliced apples or pears with thin sliced low-fat cheese. This is a good choice for children with loose teeth.

- Grapes or cherries are fun and easy to eat. Do not give fruits with pits to kids under 5. This includes cherries, peaches, and dates.

Dairy

- Choose milk that says reduced fat, low-fat, skim, non-fat, or fat-free on the label.

- Cheese is part of the milk food group. Put sliced low-fat or non-fat cheese in sandwiches. String cheese is a good choice for a lunch bag.

- Choose yogurt that says low-fat or non-fat on the label.

- A little frozen yogurt once in a while is a good choice for dessert. Make sure it is low-fat or non-fat. Check the amount of sugar in each serving.

Proteins

- Choose meats that don't have a lot of fat you can see. Sliced turkey, lean roast beef, or chicken are good choices. Serve these in a sandwich with whole-grain breads. Roll up meat with a piece of thin sliced low-fat cheese.

- Cut thin slices from leftover dinner meats such as roasts, whole chickens, or turkey to make sandwiches. Be sure to cut away fats.

- Chop up leftover turkey or chicken from dinner and make chicken salad or turkey salad sandwiches. Make the turkey or chicken salad with a little non-fat mayo or mustard.

- Eggs are in the meat and beans group. Hard boil an egg for lunch.

- Use nuts and seeds. Walnuts and almonds are good for snacks at recess and after school. **Do not give a child nuts if he or she has a nut allergy.**

- Sunflower seeds and pumpkin seeds are fun to eat. Add crushed peanuts or almonds on top of yogurt.

- Add nuts like walnuts, cashews, or pecans to a salad.

- Peanut butter can be used in a sandwich. Add mashed banana to the sandwich for a change and a treat. Spread peanut butter into celery or on apple slices.

- **Do not give your child peanut butter if he or she has a nut allergy.**

- Use pinto or black beans and lean chicken or turkey to make a burrito.

- Make chili from lean ground turkey or lean ground beef. (If you use lean ground beef, drain away any fat after you cook it.) Add kidney beans, pinto beans, black beans, or white beans. Serve with a little shredded cheese on top. Stir in some low-fat or non-fat sour cream.
- Veggie burgers are good choices in this food group. Serve on a toasted English muffin with hummus.

What can I do?

- Make sure your child eats what you put in their lunch.
- Let them help choose the food that goes into their lunch.
- If your children do not like what you pack, they may throw it out, trade with someone for less healthy food, or eat less healthy foods from the cafeteria. Talk to your children after school. Ask them what they ate. Ask what they liked. Ask them for their ideas on how to make their lunches more tasty and healthy.

When should I get help?

- If your child is not eating his or her lunch. See a dietitian for ideas. The school usually has a dietitian who may have ideas. Ask your doctor or nurse.

Healthy Drinks

What is it?

Healthy drinks are the healthy liquids babies and children drink. Healthy drinks do not have a lot of sugar. They are better choices than sugary soft drinks and fruit juice with lots of added sugar.

Did you know?

- Some drinks like juice have a lot of sugar. They are not good for the health of your child. They may make your child heavy. If you drink fruit juice, be sure it says "100% fruit juice." Add a little water to the juice. Only serve a little in a small glass. Give your children whole fruit instead.

- Fruit punch is bad for kids. It has a lot of sugar. Some are called fruit drinks. Fruit punch and fruit drinks are not good for your child.

- Water is a very good drink for children age 1 or older.

- Babies under 1 year can also drink water. They do not need water if they are breastfeeding (nursing) or drinking formula. Give a baby water only if it is very hot outside and the baby looks like he or she needs more water.

- Water from your sink may have fluoride in it. Fluoride will help your children's teeth. You will not see the fluoride but it may be there. Bottled water does not have fluoride in it unless it says so on the bottle.

- Do not give soft drinks (soda pop) to kids. Soft drinks are not good for kids. They have too much sugar and can make your child heavy. Soft drinks will harm your child's teeth.

What can I do?

- Here are some healthy choices for drinks.

Milk

- Breast milk is the best thing for babies to drink in the first 12 months.
- Babies from birth to 12 months old should have breast milk or formula. They should not have milk from a store or other liquids like juice or soda.
- Some moms cannot be home to nurse their baby. If you cannot be home, you can pump breast milk and put it in bottles and then give it to your baby. Ask your nurse or doctor how to do this. You can buy or rent a pump.
- Between age 1 and 2, ask your doctor or nurse if you should give whole milk or low-fat milk. After age 2, use low-fat milk. Ask your doctor or nurse if this is a good choice for your child.

Water

- At age 1, children can begin to drink water.
- Tap water from the sink is safe to drink in most places. Check with your city to see if your tap water is safe to drink.
- Tap water can be put in the refrigerator to get cold. Cold water may taste better to your child.

- Kids need more water when it is hot outside and they play a lot and sweat.
- Many foods have water in them like grapes, peaches, watermelon, and oranges. These are good foods for children to eat and will add water to kids' bodies.

Soft drinks (soda pop) and fruit juice

- Do not give children soft drinks. If you do give a child a soft drink, it should be a diet soda. Regular soft drinks have about 10 spoons or more of sugar. This can make your child heavy.
- Fruit juice should be 100% juice with no added sugar. If you give your child juice that is not 100%, mix one-half water with one-half juice.
- If you give your child juice or soft drinks, it should be just a little and not often. Kids can have juice or soft drinks on holiday or once in a while.

When should I get help?

- You stop breastfeeding (nursing). Check with your doctor or nurse about what you should do.
- You do not know how to pump breast milk.
- You need to buy or rent a pump to pump breast milk. Ask your doctor or nurse how to store breast milk and how to warm it after it has been in the refrigerator. They can help you or tell you where to get help.
- Your child will not drink water and only wants juice or soft drinks. Talk to your doctor or nurse about what you can do.

Snacks

What is it?

A snack is a small amount of food your child eats between meals and before bedtime. A healthy snack is food that has nutrients that are good for your child's health.

Did you know?

- Good snacks will give your child energy during the day.
- Snacks can help you feel full and not get too hungry before a meal.
- Snacks can be healthy.
- Healthy snacks will help give your heavy child vitamins and minerals.
- Sweet snacks like candy, cake, chips, and cookies should not be given to kids every day. Use them once in awhile as a special treat. Give them only a small amount when you do.
- Most vending machines do not have healthy snacks. If there is no other choice, choose things like pretzels, Fig Newtons, fruit, any kind of nuts, yogurt, or anything that is low fat. Do not choose chips or fried snacks.
- Sweet drinks such as soda or juice are not healthy. Water is the best thing to drink. Juice has a lot of sugar in it and is not healthy unless it is 100% juice.
- Choose healthy snacks as part of the day's meal plan.

- Do not allow snacks within 2 hours of meals.

- When shopping, let children pick snacks like cheese, fruits, and veggies. Let children help pick the snacks that they like. Use this time to teach your children about healthy snacks.

- Put healthy snacks in the same place where they are easy to reach. Put them in the fridge or in a corner of the counter. Cut up fruits and veggies and keep them in an easy to reach place in the fridge.

- Children should be given snacks around the same time each day. Give children snacks when they give up naps or at 10 in the morning and 3 in the afternoon. Children will make a habit out of having a snack at these times.

- Never use a snack as a reward for doing something right.

- Children should not eat snacks just for something to do when they are bored.

- Children need healthy snacks to help with hunger between meals.

- Children should only snack when they are hungry. A snack should be one serving. Do not let it become a meal.

- Have children sit at the table to eat a snack. Do not let children walk around the house or play when they eat. Do not let them snack while watching TV. They may eat a lot more than they should, because they are not paying attention.

- Some kids may get sick after eating some foods like peanuts or eggs. This is called a food allergy. If your child has a food allergy, do not give your kid foods that he or she is allergic to. Do not give children foods that have their allergic foods in them, such as peanut butter or breads that have been made with eggs or nuts. Children could also be allergic to strawberries or other foods.

- Snacks can have lots of salt in them. Salt is called sodium on the label.

- Some kids do not want snacks. They may grow out of needing snacks. This is OK. Never force a kid to eat a snack if he or she is eating 3 healthy meals a day.

What can I do?

- Prepare snacks ahead of time. Snacks should be easy to get to and ready to eat. Put one serving in a plastic bag or wrap so they are ready to eat at snack time.

- Leftover food from dinner or lunch can be a healthy snack.

- Put an extra snack in your child's lunchbox to take to school. Then your children can have a healthy snack after school or if they go to a friend's house.

- Most fruits are healthy. Fruits are sweet and can be served whole, sliced, cubed or in wedges. Canned, frozen, and dried fruits may be healthy if no sugar is added. Some healthy fruits are:

  - Apples
  - Berries
  - Cherries
  - Apricots
  - Cantaloupe
  - Grapefruit

Snacks

- Grapes
- Kiwis
- Mangoes
- Oranges
- Pears
- Strawberries
- Honeydew
- Oranges
- Nectarines
- Peaches
- Plums
- Watermelon

- Applesauce with no sugar added is easy to serve and healthy.

- Dried fruit should have no sugar added.

- Freezing grapes or other berries is easy.

- Get children to help make fruit salad and then leave it in the refrigerator. Use all kinds of fruit with lots of colors. Put the fruit salad in a single-serving-size bowl or plastic bags.

- Veggies are also healthy and can be served raw or with a dip. Some healthy veggies include:

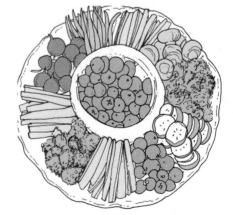

  - Carrot sticks or baby carrots
  - Broccoli
  - Cauliflower
  - Celery sticks
  - Cucumbers
  - String beans
  - Tomato slices

- Dips should be low-fat. Look for store-bought dips or dressings. Make your own from yogurt or low-fat mayo.

Snacks

- Breads, cereal, and muffins that are whole grain are more healthy than other kinds. Choose ones that are low in fat and sugar.

- Yogurt can be a healthy snack if it is low-fat or non-fat. There are many kinds of yogurt. Yogurt can be fun to eat. Make sure it does not have too much sugar.

- Water is a healthy drink.

- Low-fat milk and fat-free milk are healthy also. They come in single-serving boxes or larger. Make sure your children can pour milk into a glass or tell them to get help pouring.

- Fruit juice should be 100% juice with no added sugar. Do not give children fruit juice that has a small amount of fruit and lots of added sugar.

When should I get help?

- Your child is eating too many snacks and won't eat at mealtime.

- Your child only wants sugar snacks like cookies and candy.

- You need ideas for healthy snacks. Ask the doctor or nurse. Ask the school dietitian. They may have ideas to give you.

- Your child eats small amounts of food all day long.

- Your child keeps gaining weight.

Fast Food

What is it?

Fast food is food from outside the home that is cheap and ready to eat. You can buy the food from a drive-through lane. Fast food smells good. You get it quick. It is sometimes fun to eat. Burgers, tacos, and fried chicken are kinds of fast food.

Did you know?

- Eating at a fast food restaurant should not take the place of eating at home with the family. The home-cooked family meal is still the best kind of meal.
- Fast food can be high in calories, salt, and bad fat.
  - French fries, milk shakes, and fried food are very high in fat.
- Food ads seen by kids show foods that are fun to eat and give a prize to kids. Kid meals often come with a toy.

- Kids do not think about healthy food when they choose foods at a restaurant. They like the ones they see on TV or the ones their friends talk about.

- Double cheeseburgers, extra-large fries, or super-size meals add calories that your heavy child does not need.

- Many fast food restaurants now have healthy choices on their menus. Ask the person who takes your order about healthy choices.

- Choose foods that are lower in calories and fat.

- Check the food. How it is cooked? How many calories are in the food? How much fat is in the food? Ask to see a nutrition info sheet.

- Kids who eat in fast food restaurants tend to eat fast food for the rest of their lives.

- Try not to go to a fast food restaurant more than once a week. Let your children know why. Tell them it is not to punish. It is because much of the food served there is not good for their health.

- Look at what is in the kid's meal to see if it is healthy. The meal for a kid may not be as healthy as an adult meal.

What can I do?

- Try to order healthy foods at fast food restaurants. Do not order foods that have a lot of calories, fat, or salt. Ask how the food is made. Ask for the nutrition info sheet. This will tell you calories, fat, and other things about each food.

- Do not add salt, sauce, or dressings to the food. Order the food and ask for no sauces, or sauce on the side of the food, so you can add a small amount to the food. Small amounts of ketchup and mustard are OK to add.

- Ask for the food you want the way you want it. If you want no sauce or toppings, ask for that. Most restaurants will serve your meal how you want it.

- Order a small size. Never order large or super-large.

- Eat slowly. You will eat less food this way. You will know when you are full.

- Order from the kid's menu even for older children because the size of the meal is smaller. Order a half portion or have 2 kids share a meal.

- See what is in the kid's meal and make sure it is healthy. A kid's meal with French fries is not healthy. Ask the counter person for the toy and sometimes they will give it to you. Ask if you can have fruit or a salad in place of French fries.

- Drink water. A diet soda as a special treat once in awhile is OK. Non-fat milk or low-fat milk are also healthy choices. Do not drink juice or regular soda.

- Be careful not to make healthy food choices into unhealthy food by adding topping or dips. Apples are healthy, but the caramel dip is not healthy. Ask the counter person to hold the dip or throw it away.

- Do not go to all-you-can-eat restaurants. These are also called "buffet" restaurants. There is no portion control, and the food can be not healthy. Your family will eat too much because there are so many things to taste.

- Some ways to make eating at fast food restaurants more healthy are:
  - Ask for whole wheat bread for sandwiches.

- Order salad with the dressing put on the side. Only use half of the dressing.

- Order a small burger or sandwich with no mayo, sauce, or cheese.

- A grilled chicken sandwich is better than a burger.

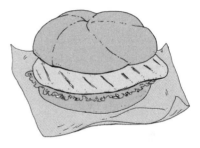

- Only eat one slice of bread or one side of the bun.

- Do not order anything that is fried.

- If you feel full and have not finished your meal, take the rest of the food home.

- Use low-fat dressings.

- Do not use gravy.

- Ask the restaurant to give you veggies or fruit instead of fries. Many times they will do this at no extra charge.

- Bring some healthy food to the restaurant with you and use it instead of unhealthy choices. If your child has a hamburger, give your child apples or other fruit instead of fries. Carrots and celery taste good with a hamburger.

- Try not to order desserts. If you order desserts, share them. Bring a more healthy dessert with you.

When should I get help?

- Your heavy child cries because they can't have French fries or other unhealthy food at a fast food restaurant.

- Your heavy child only likes to eat at fast food restaurants.

Having a Healthy Lifestyle

Notes

_____

_____

_____

_____

_____

_____

_____

_____

_____

_____

_____

_____

Exercise

What is it?

Exercise is moving around, playing, and being active.

Did you know?

- Everyone should move around and exercise.
- Exercise helps kids grow up with strong muscles and bones.
- Exercise is a good way to keep your child at a healthy weight.
- There are 3 kinds of exercise:
  - The kind that makes you sweat and breathe hard and makes your heart beat fast, like running, skating, swimming, or playing basketball or tennis.
  - The kind that builds up your muscles, like push-ups, sit ups, and lifting weights.
  - The kind that stretches you and makes your body able to bend better, like yoga, stretching, dancing, or karate.
- Kids should do a total of at least 1 hour of exercise each day.
- Here is a plan for a child to do 1 hour of exercise in a day:
  - Clean own room for 10 minutes
  - Ride bike for 10 minutes
  - Soccer practice for 20 minutes

- Walk the dog with Dad for 15 minutes
- Take out trash for 5 minutes

- There are many things that count as exercise:
  - Play games like tag
  - Ride a bike
  - Dance
  - Play on the swing set and monkey bars
  - Jump rope

- Chores count as exercise, too. These things all count as exercise:
  - Cut the lawn
  - Sort and fold laundry
  - Sweep, dust, vacuum
  - Take out the trash
  - Make beds

- Kids who exercise sleep better. Sleep helps your child learn better in school.

- Sports are a great way for your child to get exercise. Be sure your child is checked by a doctor or nurse before starting a sport.

- If your child does not like to be on a sports team have your child exercise alone or with a friend.

- - Play catch with a baseball or football
  - Shoot baskets at the park
  - Run and kick a soccer ball
- Some kids are worried about being on a team and not doing well. Look for teams that do not keep score. They focus more on playing and having fun.

What can I do?

- Make sure your child gets enough exercise. To start, play games with them where they have to walk and run.
- Do not let your child do too much exercise at one time. Your child is doing the right amount of exercise when your child can still talk while exercising.
- **If your child feels faint, sick, or dizzy when they exercise, stop and let them rest. Call 9-1-1 if they have chest pain, pass out, or cannot breathe.**
- Do not let your child spend all of his or her free time watching TV, playing video games, or on the computer.
- Go for walks with your child. A walk around the block is good exercise.
- Have your child walk the dog. Offer to walk a neighbor's dog if you do not have a dog. Make sure this is safe first. Be sure your child can handle the dog. Be sure the dog does not bite.
- Walk with your child to the store.

- Park your car far away from the entrance to the store. This will make you and your child walk more.

- Let your child push the cart at the grocery store.

- Take the stairs instead of the elevator. Make a contest of how many stairs you take each day.

- Talk to a coach when your child wants to play sports. Ask about how they run the team. Look for a team that plans for kids to have fun. Look for a team where a kid can learn a sport. Stay away from teams that only want to win.

When should I get help?

- Your child wants to play a sport. Get an okay from your doctor or nurse first.

- You are not sure what kinds of exercises are right for your child. Ask a coach or fitness counselor at school.

- You are not sure how much exercise your child should do each day.

- Your child has an injury that keeps him or her from doing exercise.

- Other children on a team make fun of your child for being heavy. Talk to the coach or the parents of other kids.

Sports

What is it?

Sports are a way kids can be active and get exercise. Sports can be fun. They can be hard to do for some kids. They can also help your child get into good shape and not be heavy. Sports can be a way for kids to make new friends and be busy in a good way.

Did you know?

- Sports are ways in which groups of kids play a game together as a team. Some team sports are:
  - Baseball
  - Basketball
  - Football
  - Hockey
  - Soccer
  - Softball
  - Tennis

- Other kinds of sports are done alo Some of these sports are:
  - Cycling
  - Gymnastics
  - Karate

- Running
- Skateboarding
- Skating
- Skiing
- Swimming
- Track and field

- Sports are a good way for your child to be with other kids and make friends.

- Most sports give your child a good way to move around. This is good for their heart and muscles.

- Kids can play sports in teams or with friends just for fun. Some teams are at schools. Some teams are in your city.

- Team sports give kids a way to reach goals for themselves. They help them learn to prepare and work on shared goals.

What can I do?

- Let your child choose which sports and games he or she wants to play. Show your child many kinds of sports. Ask your child which ones he or she likes.

- Be sure the sport is right for your child's age, size, and ability. For some sports, your child needs to have special skills. For baseball or softball, your child has to be able to throw, hit, and catch a ball. For basketball, your child needs to run and bounce a ball at the same time, and shoot the ball into the basket.

- For some sports kids need special shoes, clothes, and a lot of stuff. This can cost a lot of money. Be sure your child plays the sport first and likes it. Then you will not spend money on things your child will not use. Make sure you can afford the uniform and equipment.

- Talk with your child about what he or she likes about the sport. Ask what they don't like. Make sure the sport is a good fit for your child.

- Do not force your child to play a sport. Some parents want their child to play a sport because they played it when they were kids. Your child may not enjoy the sport.

- Be sure your child is safe playing the sport. If your child is slow or small he or she should not be in a team sport where the other children are bigger and faster. This is true in sports where contact is part of the game, like football, basketball, or hockey.

- Talk to your child's doctor before your child starts in a sport.

- Make time for your child to practice each week. Some practice will be with the team. Your child should practice on the parts of the game that they do not do well. Help your child with these parts. This will help with your child's confidence.

- If your child is a part of a team and is unhappy, talk to the coach. Work with the coach to help your child have a better time.

When should I get help?

- Your child has an injury.
- Your child is not doing well in the sport and it is affecting their self esteem.
- The coach of the team will not let your child play.
- You are not sure if a sport is right for your child's age and size.

Sleep

What is it?

Sleep is when you are out when you go to bed. Sleep helps our minds and bodies "recharge" so they work better. It is like when you plug in your cell phone when the battery is low. It helps your child's body grow and be healthy.

Did you know?

- Kids who get the right amount of sleep have less of a chance to be heavy.

- Good sleep helps your child do better in school. Things they learned in school are stored as memory during sleep. They will remember more of the things they learned that day.

- The right amount of sleep will help your child feel good. They will be in a better mood if they get enough sleep.

- Sleep helps keep us healthy and helps our body fight off being sick.

- Many kids have sleep problems once in a while. Visit your doctor if your child often:
  - Does not fall asleep.
  - Wakes up many times at night.

- Has nightmares or wakes up crying or screaming.

- Wets the bed after he or she uses the potty.

- Babies less than a year old may need 15 hours or more of sleep each day.

- Kids ages 1 to 3 years need 12 or more hours of sleep each day. This includes nap times.

- Kids ages 3 to 12 need 10 or more hours of sleep each night.

- Kids ages 12 to 18 need about 9 hours of sleep each night.

- Kids are all different. Some kids may need more or less sleep. This is OK.

What can I do?

- Make bedtime and going to sleep a habit. Do the same thing every night. This way your child will know what to expect and will sleep better.

  - Have a light, healthy snack.

  - Give your child a bath.

  - Put on your child's pajamas.

  - Have them brush their teeth.

  - Read your child a bedtime story, or have your child read a story to you.

  - Make sure the room is dark and not too warm or cool.

  - Leave on a dim night light if your child does not like the room too dark.

  - Say good night and leave the room.

- Do not let your child have a TV in his or her room. Do not let your child use the computer after bedtime. They may stay up very late watching TV or using the computer to play video games.

- Do not watch a scary movie or read scary stories before bedtime.

- Do not give your child anything with caffeine in it before bedtime. Caffeine is in soft drinks, coffee, tea, chocolate, hot cocoa, and energy drinks. Do not give your child anything with a lot of sugar in it.

- Have your child quiet down to get ready for sleep. Ask your child to sit, read, or rest about an hour before getting ready for bed. Do not let your child exercise or run around before bedtime. This will make it hard for your child to go to sleep.

- The bed should be used just for sleep. Kids will sleep better if they do **not** do these things in bed:

  - Talk on the phone
  - Do homework
  - Play video games

When should I get help?

- Your child does not sleep enough each night.

- Your child wets the bed, has nightmares, or wakes up many times during the night.

- You are not sure how much sleep your child should get.

Computer, TV, and Video Games

What is it?

Sitting and watching TV, playing video games, and using the computer.

Did you know?

- Kids who eat while watching TV eat more food. They are not thinking about the food they eat. This can lead to eating too much food.

- TV, computers, and video games are part of many kids' lives. Exercise and playing games where you have to move around should also be a part of your child's life.

- Video games have ratings. Look at these ratings to see if the game is OK for your child's age. Some video games have a lot of violence, like bloody fights, guns, knives, bombs, hurting, and killing. These games are popular, but they do not give a good message to kids. Find games that teach your child something positive, like helping people or learning.

Video game ratings

- Check websites that your child likes. The sites should be for doing homework, for learning, or for things that you talk about with your child and approve. There are many websites that are not good for children. Some sites, called chat rooms, let your child "talk" with strangers. This can be bad for your child.

What can I do?

- Do not let your child watch TV, use the computer, or play video games for more than 2 hours each day. Children under 2 years old should not watch TV.

- Do not put a computer or TV in your child's room. You will not be able to tell how much your child is using them. Put the computer or TV where you can see how much your child is using them and what they are watching.

- Watch TV with your child. This helps make it family time. You can also be sure that the shows your child watches are good choices.

- Talk with your child about video games. Have your child tell you about the game. Ask them how they feel about the game.

- Play video games alone before you let your child play them. Then you will know if they are bad games or have bad parts in them.

- Computers can let you know what websites or games your child uses. These programs can also control how long your child can use the computer each day. You can type in "parental control" on your computer web browser or the help box. Ask your child to help you do this. Let them know you want to be sure they are using the computer for good things. Let them know you want to protect them.

- Turn off the TV during mealtimes or while your child does homework. TV can make it hard for your child to think and learn while doing homework. Focus on your meal and your family at mealtime.

- Tell your children they must earn their time watching TV or using computer or video games. You can say they must do their chores and homework before they watch TV or use the computer. Give them points for doing exercise. They can use these points for TV or computer time.

When do I need to get help?

- You need to learn how to use a computer.
- You don't know how to use the parental controls on your TV or computer.
- You don't understand the ratings on TV shows or video games.
- Your child acts bad or mean after playing video games.
- Your kid won't follow your rules for TV, computer and video games.

Friends

What is it?

Kids need other kids as friends. Kids need friends who help them live a healthy life. A friend may talk your child into eating carrots instead of candy. This is healthy. A friend may talk your child into eating ice cream and cake. This may not be healthy.

Did you know?

- A friend who is the same age as your child is called a "peer."
- When friends try to get your child to do something it is called "peer pressure."
- Kids need to learn how to have friends.
- Kids need to know how to say "no" to things they should not do.
- Family is more important than friends. Family can help kids fight peer pressure and do the right thing.
- Being part of a group and having friends is important to kids as young as 7 years old.
- Kids want to look and act like everyone else. They want to fit in. Kids do not want to look different.
- Beauty on TV is about how a person looks. Let your children know that real beauty is being healthy, smart, a helper, a friend, and a good child.

- Heavy kids get teased and bullied a lot by other kids.

- Teasing and not being a part of a group can cause a kid to feel bad.

- Kids tease and bully other kids because they feel bad about themselves. Sometimes making another kid feel bad makes the teaser feel better.

- True friends are there for you no matter how you look.

- Kids who are being teased or bullied are unhappy. They may not tell you. Signs that a kid might be unhappy are:

  - Looks sad
  - Doesn't want to go out with other kids
  - Always wants to be at home
  - Tries to get out of going to school
  - Finds things that he or she can do alone, like watching TV or playing video games
  - Says he or she is sick a lot of the time

What can I do?

- Talk to your children about peer pressure. Practice how to say "no" to other kids.

- Teach kids about healthy eating. Practice what they can say if kids are trying to get them to eat junk food.

Friends

- Talk to your child about health and feeling good, not about looks. It is better for your child's health to have less fat around the waist.

- Don't talk about going on a diet. Talk about being healthy and making good choices.

- If your child is being teased or bullied, practice what your child could say to the other kids. Your kid can say something like, "That really hurts when you say that." Your child can also just walk away, ignore the teaser, or just get new friends.

- If the teasing or bullying does not stop, you can talk to the teaser's parents or teacher. Make a plan with other adults to help stop the teasing and bullying.

- When your child is eating at a friend's house, you might:
  - Give your child a healthy snack before he or she leaves the house. This will help them to not be hungry. They will not eat unhealthy snacks at the friend's house.
  - Teach children about the amount of food to eat or portion size. Teach kids which foods to skip, like those that are high in calories or fat.

- Don't get angry at a child who eats poorly. Talk about healthy eating habits with your child. Talk with your child about how you can both stick to healthy eating. This is how your child needs to eat for the rest of his or her life.

- It does not work if kids are always saying "no" to favorite foods. At times, allow a small serving of a favorite food that is high in calories. Be sure your child understands why you are doing this. It is a treat, not a reward.

Friends

- Put a healthy snack in your child's backpack or pocket to eat if he or she gets hungry. This stops poor eating at vending machines or fast food places.

- Help your children shop for clothes that look good on them. There are clothes and colors that make you look thin. Some clothes and colors make you look heavy. Dark colors are good to wear when you are heavy. Patterns like plaids or polka-dots are not good.

- Help your child have nice friends. Good friends support your child. Kids who tease or bully other kids are not good friends. They can make your child feel bad.

When should I get help?

- If your child is being teased or bullied, talk to the other child's parents, teachers, or counselors at school.

- If your child is feeling bad, talk to a doctor or nurse.

Family 6

Family Support

What is it?

Family support is when the whole family helps your heavy child eat and live healthy. Family includes the mom and dad, sisters and brothers, and anyone else who lives in the home. Grandma and grandpa, aunts and uncles, or cousins who live in the home are all family. Close friends or babysitters who live in the home also may be family.

Did you know?

- Losing weight should not be the main thing in a family even when a child is heavy. A healthy lifestyle includes eating right, doing exercise, and having support and love from the family. Everyone in the family should be a part of this.

- Mom and dad and all the adults in a family must show your child how to eat healthy. All the adults should eat right, exercise, and love the children. A healthy lifestyle does not include smoking, drinking beer or booze, or using swear words.

- It takes time for a family to learn to eat right and live healthy. Don't expect big changes to happen fast. Keep doing what will help your heavy child.

- It is important for you to learn which foods are right for your child and the whole family.

- Kids may not always want to live a healthy lifestyle. They may sneak candy or cookies or skip a walk. It is important not to get mad at them. It is better to give them support than to scold them.

- Start your children eating healthy as soon as they begin to eat solid food. Don't give your children junk food. Don't give your children food or drinks that are high in calories, fat, and sugar.

- It is important to help your children feel good about who they are. The family needs to help and support each other. This builds your children's self-esteem. Kids who feel good about themselves are more likely to live healthy lifestyles.

- Families should trust, respect, and love each other. Families who do this are more likely to have healthy and happy children.

What can I do?

- The whole family should eat healthy and exercise. This includes children who are heavy and children who are not heavy.

- Adults need to live a healthy lifestyle so their children will learn to have a healthy lifestyle.

- Do not use the word "diet." Talk about healthy eating. You get to the right weight by living a healthy lifestyle. This matters more than looking good.

- Have a family meeting about a healthy lifestyle. Include all those who live in the house. Talk about changes in eating and exercise. During the family meeting you can discuss things like:

  - Supporting each other

  - Making good choices

  - Foods that are healthy

  - Snacks that can be eaten between meals

  - Weight goals. Writing these goals on a piece of paper that can be seen may help. This can help kids look at their goals and see how close they are to getting to their goals.

  - How to exercise together or alone

  - Not to call anyone names

  - The times for meals like dinner

  - Each person's job at mealtime. These include helping cook, clean up, or setting the table.

  - When is the next family meeting

- Have food and eating rules. Let the whole family know the rules. Rules can be:

  - No junk food like candy, cake, or cookies

- No eating with the TV or radio on
- Eating should be at the table
- Families should talk during meals
- Families should not eat fast and rush through dinner
- No soft drinks, fruit juice that is not 100% fruit, or other sugar drinks

• No one should nag about eating the right food. If kids eat something that is not healthy, talk to them. Give them support to start to eat healthy.

• When you have a heavy child, talk to the child's sisters and brothers. Get them to support your heavy child. Explain how important it is to help each other. The sisters or brothers may not want to help the child. They may tease your heavy child. If a sister or brother says something like:

"I don't want to be seen with her since she is so fat. My friends make fun of her and then I feel bad."

You can then say something like this:

"She is trying to make healthy choices and we all have to help her. We must give her support by telling her what a good job she is doing. Maybe you can go on a walk with her without your friends around. We all need to be kind and help her. The family has to stick together. It will help us all. Do you think you can do that?"

- Go on a family walk as often as you can. Talk to your children about how their day was. Talk about things that are going on at school and in your home.

- Have the family shop for food together. Look at labels and buy healthy foods. Teach your family about food shopping.

- Every once in a while let kids have a bit of some foods they don't eat. This should not happen often, but once in a while it is OK. For example, if grandma and grandpa visit and bring cookies, it is OK to let your child have one.

- If your child wants a sweet dessert after a meal or candy before bedtime, suggest other healthy food. Instead of saying no, say "How about some yogurt or carrots?" Or ask your child, "Can you think of something that is more healthy for you?" Try to talk about other things to get your child's mind off of food.

- Teach children about healthy foods and a healthy life. Talk to your children while fixing dinner. Talk about being healthy during dinner.

- Praise children for their effort. Do this even if you don't see a weight change. A healthy lifestyle is important.

- Older children may find it useful to keep a journal.

- A journal is a blank book that the child writes in.
- The child tells what happened that day and what food they ate.
- Read the journal with your child. Talk about what was good and not good.
- Families can write goals they want to reach.
- Family goals can be for behavior change, healthy foods, and exercise. Goals can be:
  - Do not buy any sugar drinks.
  - Buy carrots and celery for snacks.
  - Walk one half mile every day.
  - Take children food shopping.
- Talk to your doctor or nurse about using a journal.

When should I get help?

- Your family won't support your heavy child. Talk to your doctor, nurse, or teacher.
- You need to learn about healthy foods and how to cook them. Talk to your doctor or nurse. They may send you to a dietitian.
- Your child will not eat the right foods. Talk to your doctor or nurse.
- You think your child needs more help than you can give.

Food as Reward

What is it?

Some people use food as a reward for their children. They give kids sweets or fatty foods when they do well in school or have good behavior.

Did you know?

- Rewards are given to let children know they did something good. Rewards help good behavior become a habit. When it is a habit, you do not need to reward it any more.

- Food is meant to give your body what it needs to stay healthy and strong. Food should not be given as a reward.

- Giving food as a reward may confuse your child. Your child will not understand that you only eat food for health.

- It sends a wrong message when you give your children snacks and foods that are not healthy. It tells your children that sweets and fatty foods are OK.

- You should eat food when you are hungry. Eat at mealtimes or eat a healthy snack in between meals. Food as a reward teaches your children that it is okay to eat for other reasons.

Food as Reward

- Food given as a reward connects junk food and feeling happy. This will make it harder for your child to eat healthy as an adult.

- If you give food as a reward now it will take time to change. Reward good behavior using the ideas below. Be sure you do this all the time. This will help your child get the right message. The change will take some time. Stick with it. It is worth it.

What can I do?

- Do not use food as a reward. Not even healthy food.

- Talk to your child's teachers. Make sure they do not give candy or food as a reward at school.

- Here are some rewards you can use for good behavior:

  - Think of things your child likes and use these as rewards. Going to a movie, riding in the front seat of the car, extra hugs and kisses, or listening to music. Use these things as rewards.

  - More family time together. Make time for a Family Game Night. The reward could be choosing which game to play.

- Praise your children when they do something good. Do this in front of friends and the rest of the family.

- Put a note or sign on the fridge that says what your child did well. Add a star or sticker to it each time they do it well again.

- A trip to the library, park, or playground is a healthy reward.

- Read an extra bedtime story.

- Buy stickers and give them to your children when they do well.

- Get some small things that your child likes that don't cost much.
  Go to the dollar store and pick up things like stickers, pencils, and other little things. Put them in a box. When your children do something well, they get to take one thing from the box. Let your children decorate the box.

- For older children, you can give them play money. Write up a list of what they get for the money when they earn enough. Here are some ideas:

  - Game or movie rentals
  - A book or CD

- Stay up a half hour past bedtime on weekends
- Send extra text messages
- A half hour extra time on the computer
- Have a friend over for a sleepover

When do I need to get help?

- Your child insists on food as a reward.
- You need more ideas on what to use instead of food as a reward.

Self-Esteem

What is it?

Self-esteem is how you feel about yourself. Kids with high self-esteem feel good about who they are. They feel confident. Kids with low self-esteem don't think they are important.

Did you know?

- Kids with high self-esteem make better choices for themselves. They believe in themselves. They think that they are worth caring about.

- Kids with low self-esteem don't care about themselves. They go along with the crowd and just try to fit in. They make poor choices.

- Heavy kids are more likely to have low self-esteem. They may be teased and picked on at school. Other kids may not be friends with them. They may call a heavy kid names.

- Heavy kids may feel bad about being in sports and playing games. They may not be good at sports because of their weight. They may move slower than the other kids. Other kids may not choose them for their team in school. This can make heavy kids not want to play games and sports, even though they really need the exercise.

- Kids with low self-esteem may feel that way for the rest of their lives. It can cause many problems later in life.

- Some heavy kids with low self-esteem become sad. They may eat more because they feel bad. This only makes things worse.

What can I do?

- Tell your children you love them. This is important for children to hear from their parents.

- Do not tease heavy kids about their weight. What kids' parents think about them means a lot to them.

- Be supportive. Heavy kids are more than just their weight. They are people who have value and feelings. Let your children know that you love and care for them.

- Be a role model. It does not work to make your child eat vegetables when you are eating French fries. Make sure the whole family eats healthy.

- Do not tell your children that being heavy is good. Tell them you love them and want them to be healthy. Show support.

- Listen to what your child has to say.

- The main thing is to work with your child on a plan to eat healthy and exercise.

- Read the chapters in this book. Learn about good foods and exercise. Work with your child to be healthy.

When do I need to get help?

- Your child gets very sad (depressed) and will not do things with other people.

- Your child talks about hurting themselves.

- Your child is being picked on at school.

Restaurants

What is it?

Eating out at a restaurant (**rest**-tar-ront) is when the family goes out to eat. Food is ordered from a menu. You can usually order healthy food choices from the menu. The family pays for the meal.

Did you know?

- Eating at a restaurant is a part of an older child's social life. They may eat out with their friends. A heavy child needs to be with other kids. Learning to eat well at a restaurant is important.

- You can order healthy foods in most restaurants.

- Kids need to learn how to order healthy foods from a menu.

- Eating at a restaurant does not take the place of the family meal. It is still important to eat at home. Plan to eat at a restaurant at special times like a birthday.

- There are many kinds of restaurants. Some serve food from a culture, like Mexican, Chinese, or Thai food.

Some cost more than others. Look around to find a restaurant that fits in with the amount you can afford to spend for a meal. There are some restaurants that are as cheap as fast food.

- You do not have to eat out with your children when they are little. Kids will learn about going to a restaurant when they are older.

- It is important that you spend time with your children and talk about healthy eating and healthy food choices.

What can I do?

- Choose restaurants that have a healthy menu.

- Find out what food is served before going to a restaurant.

  - Look up a restaurant on the computer.

  - Call and ask about the food they serve.

  - Stop by a few days before you go and ask for a copy of their menu. Look over the menu and talk to your children about the healthy choices.

  - Plan what to order before you go to the restaurant.

- Try new foods at restaurants.

- Choose restaurants that serve foods that are not the same as you eat at home but are still healthy. This is a good way to have your children try new foods.

- Look over the "Kid's Menu" before eating out. A restaurant is not the best choice when the kids' menu has French fries and other fried foods. Ask if you can get salad or vegetables instead of fries with the kids' meal.

- Ask how the food is cooked. You can ask them to cook it a certain way. Some places will do this for you. Ask for meats to be cooked without oil or butter.

- Share an order of food between two kids. Share an order of food between an adult and a kid. Serving sizes can be too large for one person. Take home any leftover food.

- Water and non-fat milk or low-fat milk are the best drinks to order. Do not let your child order soft drinks or juice. Do not get refills. Give your children water if they want more to drink.

- Choose a healthy dessert such as fruit or sherbet. Have your entire family share a dessert like a piece of pie or a dish of ice cream.

- You can ask for different foods on an order. Ask for fruit or veggies in place of French fries. Many times this will be done with no added cost.

- Leave off special sauces, cheese, gravy, and whipped cream toppings. Ask for salad dressing on the side and only use half of it.

- Toddlers can't sit still until the food is served. Bring some toys or coloring books.

- Make young kids and the whole family sit at the table. Take little kids for a walk when they get restless.

- A meal that lasts more than 30 minutes may be too long for kids under 2 years old.

- Eat a piece of fruit or something else that is healthy before you go out to eat.

- You should not eat out when you are really hungry. You and the children will eat more.

- Don't add salt or butter to the meal. Restaurant food already uses a lot of salt and butter before it comes to the table.

- Start the meal with a salad. Ask the waitress to put the salad dressing to the side of the salad. Eat just enough salad dressing for taste. You may order a soup that is **not** made with cream in place of the salad.

- Eat slowly. Put your fork down between bites. Have children chew their food before taking more food. No one should talk with their mouth full of food.

- Let everyone eat until they are full. Do not make children clean their plates.

- Take home leftover food.

- Make eating at a restaurant a special time.

  - Don't do it every day.

- Talk about it and get the family excited about going to a restaurant.
- Think of things to talk about during the meal.
- Talk about things that everyone in the family would like to talk about.
- Let everyone have a chance to talk.
- Show your children how to eat healthy.
- Show your children how to have good manners.
- Make eating at a restaurant a happy and fun time.

When should I get help?

- You are not sure how to order healthy food at a restaurant.

Calling for Help

What is it?

You should get help if you do not feel like you can help your child to make healthy food choices, eat the right amount, or exercise. There are many places to go and people to talk to for help.

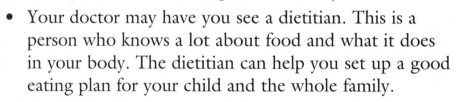

Did you know?

- Talk with your doctor and nurse about your heavy child. Tell them what you are doing. Let them know what things are hard for you to do.

- Your doctor may have you see a dietitian. This is a person who knows a lot about food and what it does in your body. The dietitian can help you set up a good eating plan for your child and the whole family.

- If your child is sad a lot or does not want to be with anyone, tell your doctor. This may be a sign of depression (dee-**presh**-un). Your doctor may send your child to another doctor called a psychologist (sie-**kol**-uh-jist). This kind of doctor will talk with your child about how your child feels. The psychologist will help your child to feel better.

- Asking for help is the sign of a good parent. Asking for help does not mean you are not smart or not a good parent.

- Your child may need a long-term program to develop a healthy lifestyle. Keep a good attitude. Help your child keep a good attitude.

What can I do?

- When you go to the doctor, write down all your questions first. Leave space on the paper for you to write down answers from the doctor or nurse. Be sure you understand all the answers. If you do not understand, tell your doctor or nurse to explain it another way so you can understand.

- Ask people for tips on cooking and eating healthy. Look in magazines and newspapers, too.

- Talk to your doctor or nurse before your heavy child joins an exercise program or a sports team. Ask how much exercise your child should do.

- If your child is being teased at school, talk to your child's teacher. If a bully is being mean to your child, talk to your child's teacher.

  - Let them know about the teasing and bullies.
  - Bullies may harm your child.
  - Tell your child to try not to pay attention to bullies.
  - Tell your child to play in groups with friends.

- Call the Weight Control Information Network. Their phone number is 877–946–4627. This is a government office. They can send you more information about how to keep your child healthy.

- If you have health insurance, ask if they have a program to help your child.

- Ask where you work if they have any programs to help your child.

When do I need to get help?

- You make changes in your family's lifestyle and eating habits but your heavy child is still gaining weight.

- You do not know what to do to keep your child healthy.

Health

7

Health Problems

What is it?

Being heavy can cause health problems. Being heavy can make your child sick. Being heavy can harm the brain, lungs, heart, blood vessels, bones, and joints.

Did you know?

- Being heavy can make kids feel bad about who they are. Your child may not be happy.
- Being heavy can also cause problems later in life:
  - Headaches and seeing double
  - Not being able to sleep
  - Shortness of breath (hard time breathing)
  - High blood pressure
  - Bleeding easy
  - Damage to blood vessels
  - Fat in the blood
  - Heart burn
  - Not being able to have a BM
  - Gallstones
  - Fatty liver
  - Pain in your joints
  - Flat feet

- Bowed knees
- Problems with your hips
- Type 2 diabetes
- Attention problems
- Skin problems
- Allergies
- Thyroid problems
- Girls may not get their period.
- Doctors do not always talk about a child being heavy.
- Treating heavy kids is hard to do.
- Many people don't try to control their child's weight.

What can I do?

- If the doctor or nurse tells you your child is heavy, believe them. Start making changes right away.
- Take steps to help your child. Read this book. Do what the book tells you to do. Talk to your doctor.

- Learn why being heavy is bad for your child's health.
- Make a plan for your heavy child and your family to eat healthy.
- Help each person in your family to be a healthy weight.
- Use this book to learn how to eat healthy.
- Use this book to learn about exercise that your child needs to do every day.
- Do not have unhealthy snacks around the house.
- Let your children shop with you. Let them pick out some healthy foods like fruits and vegetables.
- Get the whole family to do things for a healthy lifestyle.
- Ask questions. Doctors, nurses, and school counselors can help.
- Teach the whole family about a healthy lifestyle.
- Talk about your heavy child with your doctor or nurse.
- Talk about your heavy child with a teacher or a counselor at school.

When should I get help?

- You need to help your heavy child lose weight.
- You think your child has a health problem.
- Your heavy child feels bad about his or her body.

Food Allergies

What is it?

A food allergy is when the body reacts to a food that usually does not bother other people.

Did you know?

- The reasons some people have food allergies are not well known.
- Food allergies are not the child's fault or the parent's fault.
- A food allergy may make your child sick.
- There are different ways kids get sick when they have a food allergy. They may have:
  - Itchy or dry skin
  - Red bumps called "hives"
  - Rash
  - Upset stomach and vomit
  - Diarrhea
  - Runny or stuffy nose
  - Earache
  - Trouble breathing
    If your child is having trouble breathing, call the doctor or 9-1-1 right away.

Food Allergies

- Some allergies can make your child very sick. Your child may have to go to a hospital right away. Your child may have to carry an "EpiPen." The EpiPen holds a shot of medicine. If a child has a bad reaction they can give themselves the shot of medicine.

- Food allergies can be caused by different foods:

  - Shellfish like shrimp, crab, or oysters

  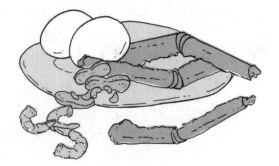

  - Fish

  - Peanuts, seeds, or tree nuts like cashews, pecans, or walnuts

  - Milk and milk products like cheese and butter

  - Eggs

  - Grains like wheat or corn

  - Soy like tofu or soy milk

  - Other foods

What can I do?

- Tell your doctor or nurse if you think your child may have a food allergy.

- Do what the doctor or nurse tells you to do for your child.

- Read food labels. Many times it will say if the food has something in it your child should not eat.

- Learn as much as you can about the different foods that may contain what your child is allergic to.
- Talk to your child about their food allergy and how to check foods before they eat them.
- Help your child choose food to stay healthy.

When should I call the doctor or nurse?

- When food has made your child sick.
- If you think your child may have a food allergy.
- If your child has an allergy and you need to know more.

Anorexia and Bulimia

What is it?

It is an unhealthy way of eating that a child cannot stop. Children who try to lose weight by doing these things may have an eating disorder.

Did you know?

- There are 2 kinds of eating disorders:
  - Eating very little food and becoming too thin. This is called anorexia (ann-oh-**rex**-ee-yuh).
  - Eating large amounts of food and then getting rid of the food by throwing up or taking laxatives. A laxative is a medicine you can buy at the drugstore that makes you have BMs. This is called bulimia (bull-**lee**-mee-yuh).
- Most people with eating problems are girls. Girls as young as 9 or 10 can have eating disorders.
- Some people who are heavy as kids become anorexic as teens.
- Most people with eating problems need help from a person who knows how to treat the disorder. Without help, the person can die.

- Only a doctor can say if your child has an eating disorder.

- People with eating disorders often have few friends. They spend a lot of time alone. They worry about food and how they look.

- Many people want to look like the movie stars they see. People on TV are very thin. If kids see these people as role models, they may want to look like them. They try to get too thin.

Your child eats too little (anorexia):

- Anorexia is a very bad illness. It starts as a diet to lose a few pounds. Once the weight is lost, your child cannot stop dieting.

- Anorexia often starts when the person is young. It can go on for many years.

- Kids with this problem eat very little. They starve themselves to be thin. They exercise a lot to get even thinner.

- Kids with this problem look very sick. Here are some signs:

  - Looks very thin, looks like just skin and bones

  - Has dry skin and thin hair

  - A girl's monthly period stops

  - Feels cold all the time

  - Pulse skips beats

  - Starts to lose teeth

- - Fine hairs grow on the arms, back, and face
  - Is weak and depressed
  - Looks sick
- Your thin child thinks that he or she is fat. Your thin child is afraid of gaining weight.
- Kids with anorexia lose their body curves. They look like very young kids again.
- The self-esteem of kids with eating disorders is tied to how thin there are. The only thing that matters is being thin.
- People with anorexia will not say that they have a problem.

Your child eats large amounts of food and throws up or takes laxatives after eating (bulimia):

- Bulimia often starts in the late teen years.
- Kids with this problem eat a lot of food in a short time. This is called binge (binj) eating. They binge alone or with friends.
- Binge eating often happens when kids feel stress. Kids also do it when they are lonely or upset.
- They eat high-calorie "junk" food like ice cream, cookies, and candy.
- They feel guilty after the binge. They make themselves throw up right after eating. They do this so they won't get fat.

- Many kids take laxatives to get the food out of their body.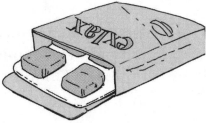

- It can be hard to tell that a kid has bulimia. The kid's weight often stays the same. Here are some signs to watch for:

  - Trips to the bathroom right after meals

  - Large amounts of food missing from the house

  - Tooth decay from throwing up often

  - Puffy face near the ears

  - Cuts and dry skin on the hands and fingers

  - Mood swings or feeling depressed

  - Pulse that skips beats

  - Muscle cramps

  - Burning in the chest

  - Feeling tired

- Kids with bulimia know they have a problem. They try to keep it a secret.

- Bulimia is a serious problem. A kid with bulimia can die without help.

What can I do?

- Eat and exercise healthy. Don't do too much exercise. Get a book to learn about healthy exercise. Teach your child about healthy eating and exercise. Talk to your doctor or nurse about how much exercise to do.

Anorexia and Bulimia

- Talk to your child about getting fit and healthy. Do not talk about being thinner. Do not talk about going on a diet. Talk about eating good food, exercise, and living a healthy life.

- Don't talk about being pretty and thin. Everyone is pretty in their own way.

- Don't ever talk about a heavy kid in a bad way. Kids should not feel shame or bad about how much they weigh.

- Serve healthy foods in the right amounts. Kids need to eat three meals and two snacks a day.

- Kids need to eat food each day from each of the food groups:
  - Whole-grain bread, cereal, rice, and pasta
  - Veggies
  - Fruits
  - Meat, poultry, fish, eggs, and nuts
  - Milk, yogurt, and cheese
  - A little bit of good fats, oil, and sweets

- Give your children foods high in iron. Foods high in iron are healthy and are needed for growing bones. Some foods high in iron are:
  - Lean meats
  - Spinach

- Raisins
- Beans
- Whole-grain cereals
- Breads with added iron

- Most people do not need to take iron pills. Healthy eating will provide you with enough iron.

- Try to eat meals together as a family.

- Teach your child healthy eating habits. Don't do these things:
  - Don't make your children eat all the food on his or her plate. Your child should stop eating when they feel full.
  - Don't use food as a reward. Don't give cake or sweets for doing well on a test.
  - Don't use food to make your child feel better. When your child is sad, talk with him or her. Eating doesn't help.
  - Don't use food to punish your child.

- Watch for signs that your child may have an eating problem.

- Don't talk about dieting around your child.

- Notice if your child goes to the bathroom right after meals.

- Take your child to the doctor if you are worried. Trust your feelings. Don't believe your child when they say they are OK if you think they are not.

When should I get help?

- Your child has lost a lot of weight.
- Your child refuses many meals.
- Your child is always on a diet. Your child is afraid to gain weight.
- Your child exercises too much.
- Your child looks sick.
- Your child has some signs of an eating problem.
- Your child is thin but says, "I'm fat."
- Your child always takes laxatives to go to the bathroom.

Diet Pills

What is it?

A diet pill is medicine to help a child lose weight. These pills can be used to make a child not want to eat, to pee more, or to have more BMs.

Did you know?

- Pills or medicine are not often given to children.
- Living a healthy lifestyle is the best way to help your child keep at a healthy weight.
- No one knows what diet pills do to your child's body after a long time. No one knows how long to use diet pills to keep the weight off.
- There are many side effects of diet pills, like stomach problems.
- There are many TV ads for losing weight by using pills you buy at the drugstore. These are called over-the-counter medicine. You can buy these without a note from the doctor. Older children and teens might buy these drugs and not tell their parents.
- Older children and teens might get these drugs at a friend's house and not tell their parents.

What can I do?

- Teach your children about healthy lifestyles. Teach your children how to eat healthy and how to exercise.

- Medicine should not be given to children unless a doctor tells you to give it. Most of the time, doctors will work with children to help them change their lifestyle.

- Tell your older children about the bad things that can happen if they take diet pills that they get at drugstore. Tell them these things can happen:
  - Higher heart rate
  - Feeling faint
  - Upsetting the balance of minerals in your body
  - Feeling sick

- Talk to your children about their daily lives.

- Watch for signs of taking diet pills.
  - See if your children are losing a lot of weight without changing the food that they eat.
  - Is your child going to the bathroom a lot?
  - Ask your children if they are taking pills to lose weight.

- Plan how you can help your children have a healthy lifestyle. Talk about food choices and more exercise. Do the things that are in this book.

- Help your child get into a weight-loss program such as Weight Watchers for kids. Find a support group for your child.

When should I get help?

- Your child is taking diet pills to lose weight.
- Your child is heavy and doesn't change what he or she eats.
- You think that your child is taking over-the-counter drugs and won't tell you.
- Your child can't stop taking over-the-counter drugs. This is called addiction, and a doctor needs to help your child.
- Your child will not stop taking diet pills.

Diabetes

What is it?

Too much sugar in the blood is a sickness called diabetes (die-uh-**bee**-tees). A blood test will show that the sugar level is too high. When there is too much sugar in the blood, the sugar gets into the pee and a test on the child's pee also shows sugar. Insulin (**in**-sue-lin) is made in your body. It helps the body to use food.

There are 2 types of diabetes:
- Type 1 diabetes
- Type 2 diabetes

Type 1 diabetes is when the body stops making insulin. Kids with Type 1 diabetes have to test their blood and take insulin shots every day. A doctor has to care for these kids.

Type 2 diabetes is when the body still makes insulin but may not make as much insulin as the body needs. People who have Type 2 diabetes have to watch their diet. They may need to lose weight. They may have to take some medicine by mouth. Insulin does not always have to be given in Type 2 diabetes. A doctor has to care for a child with Type 2 diabetes.

Did you know?

- Parents may feel bad about a child who has diabetes.
- They may feel they have done something wrong.

168

- Some parents deny that their child has diabetes. They will not take them to a doctor. These feelings are normal, but you must help if your child is sick.

- Doctors can treat diabetes, but there is no cure.

- It is important to get your child treated. This will help your child who has diabetes stay healthy.

- Diabetes in heavy children is very common.

- All heavy children should be tested for diabetes. Testing is done by a blood test when your child has not eaten for 6 hours before the test. This is called a fasting blood sugar test.

- If heavy kids lose weight, Type 2 diabetes may go away.

- Type 2 diabetes can be missed because the child may not show any signs at first.

- The bad effects of Type 2 diabetes occur over a long time.

- When a child grows up, health problems from Type 2 diabetes affect the heart, nerves, liver, kidneys, eyes, feet, and skin.

- You may see some of these when a child has Type 2 diabetes:
  - The child may be very thirsty and drinks a lot.
  - The child may pee more.
  - The child is more hungry and it may seem that the child always wants to eat.
  - Even though the child is eating a lot, he or she may lose weight.

- The child may be very tired.

- The child may be in a bad mood.

- The child may have some problems seeing. This is called blurred vision.

- The child may have sores that are slow to heal. Some cuts may not heal well.

- The child may get a lot of infections.

- The child may get patches of darkened skin around the folds in their skin. Look for this around the neck or in the armpits.

- It is hard to care for a child who has diabetes. It takes a lot of time and energy to help your child treat diabetes.

- The whole family is affected by a child who has diabetes. This includes the parents, grandparents, sisters and brothers, and others in the family. Everyone should know about diabetes and how to treat it. The family can help a child stay on the plan to treat diabetes.

- Certain things affect your child's diabetes, like colds or the flu. If your child gets sick, be sure to watch your child's diabetes by monitoring it closely.

What can I do?

- Learn as much as you can about diabetes. Read books and talk to your doctor and nurse about diabetes. Listen to people who know about this disease.

- Keeping your child healthy and preventing diabetes is the best thing a parent can do. Do these things:

  - Serve healthy foods.

- Keep your child's weight in a normal range.

- Help your child get more physical activity. Help your child get into sports, dance, or other exercise.

- Make sure your child does not watch too much TV, play video games, or use the computer all day.

- Have your child tested for Type 2 diabetes if:

  - Your child is overweight

  - A family member has diabetes

  - You are African American, Hispanic, Native American, or Asian American. These groups have a higher chance of having diabetes.

  - Your child has any of the signs of diabetes

- Treatment for Type 2 diabetes includes:

  - Blood sugar testing

  - You may have to check your child's blood 3-4 times a day.

  - This can be done through finger sticks. This is mostly for those children who have to take insulin. But it can be for those on medicine. You will learn how to do this at the doctor's office or clinic.

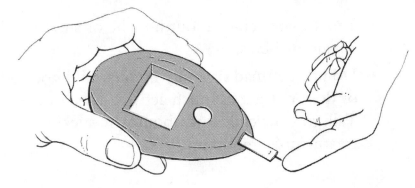

Diabetes

- Keep a paper where you write down the results of your child's blood tests. This will help your doctor know how well your child is doing.

- Eat right. Keep your child on a healthy diet that helps him or her lose weight. Cut down on the amount of sugar and high sugar foods that your child eats.

- Increase your child's activity. Help your child get into some physical activity or sport.

- Your child might be given medicine. This may include insulin, which is given by shots. Or other medicine to take by mouth. Your doctor will tell you what your child needs.

- Many children have diabetes. Get yourself and your child into a support group. Ask your doctor or nurse to help with this. The support group may be with other children who have diabetes. You all talk about common problems.

- Let the babysitter, nursery, preschool or school know if your child has diabetes. Explain the treatment plan to them so they can help your child.

- Teach your child about diabetes and what to do to treat it. Let your child select foods. Give your child healthy choices.

- Talk to your child about how he or she feels about having diabetes.

- Do not get mad or angry if your child goes off their diet or does not get as much activity as he or she should. Talk to your child and about why sticking to their treatment is important.

Diabetes

When should I get help?

- You think your child may have diabetes. See your doctor or nurse. Tell them why you think your child may have diabetes. Have your child tested.

- Your child will not follow his or her diet. See your doctor or nurse or a dietitian. Your doctor may tell you to see a counselor if your child is not following the treatment plan.

- You think your child's diabetes is getting worse. See your doctor or nurse.

- You are finding it hard to help your child. Your doctor or nurse may tell you things that will help you.

- You want to find a support group. You may become a member of a support group of parents who have children with diabetes. Your doctor or nurse can help you find these groups.

Word List

A

- **addiction**—When a person can't stop doing something that is not good for his or her health.
- **affect**—What something does to a person.
- **anorexia**—An illness where the person eats very little food and is too thin.

B

- **binge eating**—Eating extra large amounts of food in a short period of time.
- **BMI**—Body mass index; a number that tells if your weight is normal.
- **bulimia**—Eating food and then trying to get rid of the food in the body. The person may throw up or take laxatives.

C

- **calorie**—A number to measure the amount of food eaten.
- **counselor**—A person at school who can help fix problems.

D

- **depressed**—When a person is sad or unhappy all of the time.
- **diabetes**—Illness when there is too much sugar in the blood.

Word List

- **diet**—Food that we eat at meals.
- **dietitian**—A person who studies food and nutrition. Helps people with their diets.

E

- **emotion**—Strong feeling.
- **exercise**—Doing things that make you move around and improve your health.

F

- **fast food**—Food that is ready to eat when you buy it. You may buy fast food without leaving your car. You can also go in and sit down. You order food at a counter.
- **fat free**—Food that has no fat.
- **fiber**—Parts of fruits, vegetables, and grains that the body does not digest. Fiber makes you feel full longer.
- **fluoride**—A mineral that stops cavities by making teeth stronger.
- **food allergy**—Getting sick from eating one kind of a food.

G

- **generic**—Food that has the same ingredients but is not made by a name brand.
- **goal**—Something you want to do.

H

- **healthy**—Something that is good for your health.
- **hummus**—A dip made with mashed chick peas.

Word List

I

- **important**—Above everything else.

L

- **laxative**—Medicine taken to have BMs.
- **lifestyle**—How you live and what you do every day.
- **low-fat**—Food with little fat.

M

- **mineral**—Chemical found in food and needed by the body.

N

- **non-fat**—A food that does not have fat.
- **nutrition**—The sum of all things found in food and used by the body.
- **Nutrition Facts**—A label on food that lists the nutrients that are in the food.

O

- **obese**—A medical word for having too much body fat.
- **overweight**—A word for weighing too much.

P

- **parental control**—Lets a parent choose what a kid can watch on TV or do on a computer.
- **peer pressure**—Friends try to get a kid to do something. May be something good or bad.

Word List

- **popular**—Everyone thinks it is the thing to do.
- **portion**—Amount of one kind of food placed on a plate.
- **prevention**—Steps to stop something from taking place.
- **problem**—Something that needs to be fixed.
- **protein**—Found in food. Used by the body to build muscles and bones.

R

- **reward**—Giving something to a person when they do something good.
- **role model**—A person who shows good behavior that others copy.

S

- **self-esteem**—Pride that a kid feels. How they see self. Feelings of good or bad about self.
- **serving**—The amount of food that has the calories, fat, protein, fiber, and other nutrients listed on the Nutrition Facts label.
- **side effect**—What a medicine does for a body other than what you are taking it for.
- **snack**—A small amount of food. Eaten between meals.
- **starve**—To stop eating.
- **support**—Doing things to help a kid be healthy.

T

- **tease**—Making fun of a kid by calling them names that hurt.

U

- **unhealthy**—Anything that will harm the body.

V

- **veggies**—Short for "vegetables." Eat lots of these.

W

- **whole grain**—A seed that has not been broken up. Important part of a healthy diet.

What's in This Book from A to Z

What's in This Book from A to Z

What's in This Book from A to Z

What's in This Book from A to Z

People We Want to Thank

We wish to thank the following people for their help with this book:

Helen Acevez
Albert E. Barnett, M.D.
Reyna Canchola
Gina Capaldi
Blanca M. Castro
Liz Collins
Silvia Diaz
Angela Dovalina
Alberto Geddisman, M.D., MMM, CPE, FAAP
Evelia Gomez
Warren Hand
Gabriela Hernandez, BA
Patti Herrera
Yoly Herrera
Maria G. Iribarren, CN
Sharon Johnson
Rosa Ledezma
David Lee, MHA
Taina Lopez
Donna McKenzie, CFNP
Kimberly Miller, J.D.
Celia Miyamoto, M.D.
Obdulia Molina

Megan Montrone, BSN
Mai-Tram Nguyen, M.D.
Rebeca Osequera
Lynne Pantano
Barbara Price
Veronica Pulcini
Karina Quintero, BS
Gloria Ramirez-Pulcini
Pamela Ray
Ruby Raya-Morones, M.D.
Margarita Reyes
Audrey Riffenburgh, MA
Vanessa Rodriguez, BA
Nancy Rushton, RN
Duane Saikami, Pharm.D
Donna Bell Sanders, MPH
Dawn Ta, MBA
Daniel Torres
Lizzeth Vazquez, MSW
Georgina Vivanco
Diane Walker-Smith
Carolyn Wendt
Viraseni Wu, NP

Other Books in the Series

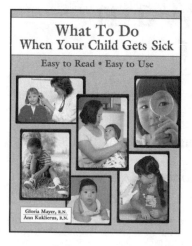

ISBN 978-0-9701245-0-0
$12.95

What To Do
When Your Child Gets Sick*

There are many things you can do at home for your child. At last, an easy to read, easy to use book written by two nurses who know. This book tells you:

- What to look for when your child is sick.
- When to call the doctor.
- How to take your child's temperature.
- What to do when your child has the flu.
- How to care for cuts and scrapes.
- What to feed your child when he or she is sick.
- How to stop the spread of infection.
- How to prevent accidents around your home.
- What to do in an emergency.

ISBN 978-0-9701245-2-4
$12.95

What To Do
For Teen Health

The teen years are hard on parents and teens. There are many things you can do to help your teen. At last, an easy to read, easy to use book written by two nurses. This book tells you:

- About the body changes that happen to teens.
- How to get ready for the teen years.
- How to talk with your teen.
- What you can do to feel closer to your teen.
- How to help your teen do well in school.
- All about dating and sex.
- How to keep your teen safe.
- The signs of trouble and where to go for help.

Also available in Spanish.
*Also available in Vietnamese, Chinese, and Korean.
To order, call (800) 434-4633.

Other Books in the Series

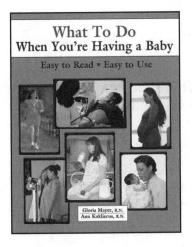

ISBN 978-0-9701245-6-2
$12.95

What To Do
When You're Having a Baby

There are many things a woman can do to have a healthy baby. Here's an easy to read, easy to use book written by two nurses that tells you:

- How to get ready for pregnancy.
- About the health care you need during pregnancy.
- Things you should not do when you are pregnant.
- How to take care of yourself so you have a healthy baby.
- Body changes you will have each month.
- Simple things you can do to feel better.
- Warning signs of problems and what to do about them.
- All about labor and delivery.
- How to feed and care for your new baby.

ISBN 978-0-9701245-4-8
$12.95

What To Do
For Senior Health*

There are many things that you can do to take charge of your health during your senior years. This book tells about:

- Body changes that come with aging.
- Common health problems of seniors.
- Things to consider about health insurance.
- How to choose a doctor and where to get health care.
- Buying and taking medicines.
- Simple things you can do to prevent falls and accidents.
- What you can do to stay healthy.

Also available in Spanish.
*Also available in Vietnamese.
To order, call (800) 434-4633.

Other Books in the Series

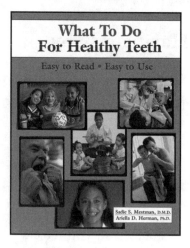

ISBN 978-0-9721048-0-9
$12.95

What To Do For Healthy Teeth

It is important to take good care of your teeth from an early age. This book tells how to do that. It also explains all about teeth, gums, and how dentists work with you to keep your teeth healthy.

- How to care for your teeth and gums.
- What you need to care for your teeth and gums.
- Caring for your teeth when you're having a baby.
- Caring for your child's teeth.
- When to call the dentist.
- What to expect at a dental visit.
- Dental care needs for seniors.
- What to do if you hurt your mouth or teeth.

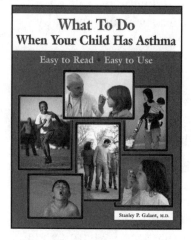

ISBN 978-0-9720148-6-1
$12.95

What To Do When Your Child Has Asthma

Having a child with asthma can be scary. This easy to read, easy to use book tells you what you can do to help your child deal with asthma:

- How to tell if your child needs help right away.
- Signs that your child has asthma.
- Triggers for an asthma attack.
- Putting together an Asthma Action Plan.
- How to use a peak flow meter.
- The different kinds of asthma medicine.
- How to talk to your child's day care and teachers about your child's asthma.
- Making sure your child gets enough exercise.
- Helping your child to take their asthma medicine the right way.
- What to do for problems like upset stomach, hay fever and stuffy nose.

Also available in Spanish.
To order, call (800) 434-4633.